Get Your Free E-book

Get Your Free E-book
Scan the QR code below to instantly access the e-book
'My Growing-Up Journal', absolutely free

https://bonus.grapevinebooks.com/growingupjournal

Contents

PUBERTY EXPLAINED FOR GIRLS 8–12

A KIND, HONEST GUIDE TO GROWING UP AND TAKING CARE OF YOU

MAREN ELLORY

Published by
GRAPEVINE BOOKS

www.grapevinebooks.com
email: contact@grapevinebooks.com

Ordering Information:

Quantity sales: Special discounts are available on quantity purchases by corporations, associations, and others. For details, reach out to the publisher.

First published by Grapevine Books 2026

Printed at New Print Services Pvt. Ltd.

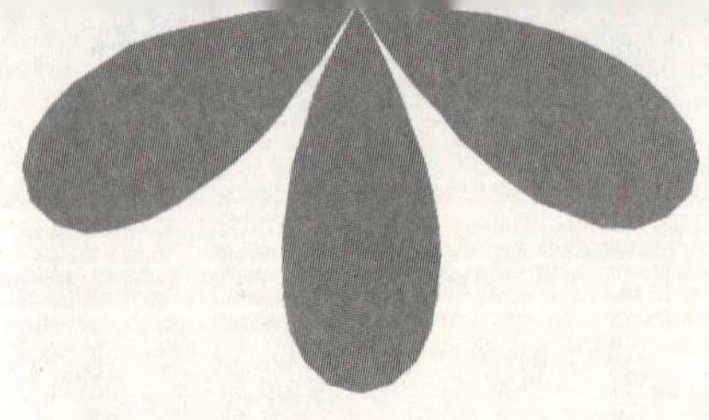

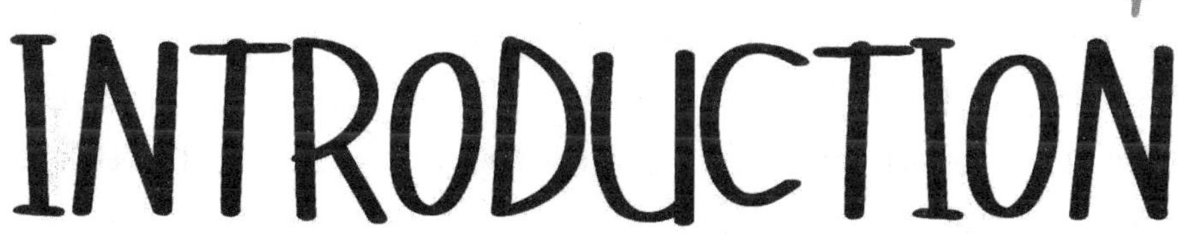
INTRODUCTION

WELCOME TO THE CLUB!

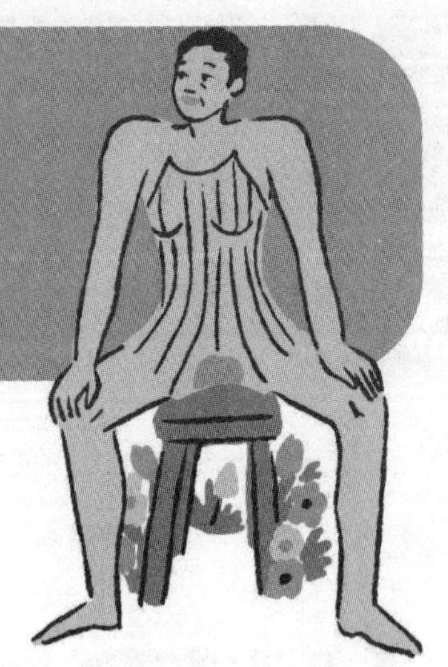

Chloe was brushing her teeth like any normal Saturday morning when she suddenly noticed something... unexpected.

"Wait, what is THAT?" she whispered, staring at the faint reddish stain in her underwear.

Panic mode: activated.

Was she hurt? Was something wrong? Should she scream? Should she text her best friend and say goodbye forever?

If you've ever had a moment like Chloe's, where your brain freezes and your heart starts pounding over a little bit of blood, take a deep breath. *You're not alone—and you are 100% not broken.*

In fact... congratulations!

You've just entered one of the coolest, weirdest, most empowering clubs out there: The Period Club. No secret handshake required, just curiosity, courage... and maybe a heating pad.

Your period is a natural part of growing up, like outgrowing your shoes overnight or suddenly noticing that you cry during shampoo commercials (it's called hormones, and yes, they're dramatic). It's not gross. It's not scary. It's just your body doing its amazing, magical thing.

And here's the deal: this book is like your older sister, best friend, and wise fairy godmother all in one. It's going to guide you through the wild world of periods—from pads to moods to the ultimate emergency kit for school days.

Ready to feel confident, calm, and kind of like a period superhero? Welcome to the club, Chloe. And welcome to the club, **YOU**.

What This Book Will Help You With

After her first period surprise, Chloe had approximately 1,000 questions. Like:

- How long is it going to last?
- What do I even use—pads, tampons, diapers??
- Am I the only one who's freaking out?

Don't worry. This book is basically a cheat code for everything you wish someone would've explained before your period popped up uninvited. *Whether you've already had your first period, think it's coming soon, or are just curious—this guide is here for it all.*

We'll talk about what a period actually is (no science mumbo-jumbo), what happens inside your body, and how you can manage it like a pro—even if it shows up during a sleepover or gym class.

You'll get real answers, product tips (nope, pads are not all the same), and total honesty about feelings, cramps, and what's actually normal.

Oh, and if you're worried about being embarrassed or messing up, *psst.* **Everyone goes through that.** Seriously. Even grown-ups forget to pack an extra pad sometimes. So it's okay to be messy, curious, or even a little nervous.

By the time you finish this book, you'll know how to handle your period without panic. You'll understand what's happening to your body and why it's nothing to be ashamed of. In fact, you'll probably feel kind of proud.

So, Chloe? She found her groove. And you will too.

EVERYONE'S TIMELINE IS DIFFERENT

Chloe's best friend, Zara, got her period at 10. Chloe was still waiting at 12. She kept checking her underwear like it was going to send her a calendar invite. "What's wrong with me?" she once whispered.

Answer: *absolutely nothing.*

Periods aren't like school bells—they don't all ring at the same time. Some people get theirs at 9, others at 14. Some grow fast, others later. That's not weird. That's just biology doing its own thing. **Your body has a unique timeline, and it's not a race.**

In fact, comparing your timeline to someone else's is like comparing apples to, well... galaxies. There's just no point!

Whether your period arrives early, late, or right on the average mark, it's totally okay. You're not behind. You're not too early. You're you.

And guess what? Once it starts, you'll realize that it's not really about when it came—it's about how you learn to care for yourself through it.

So, if your best friend is already a tampon ninja, or your cousin talks about cramps like she's been through battle, don't stress. *You're not missing out.*

And if you have gotten your period and your friends haven't yet? Be the Chloe. Be the one who says, "Don't worry, it's weird at first—but you've got this."

No matter what your start line looks like, this guide is here to walk you through the finish line with courage and kindness.

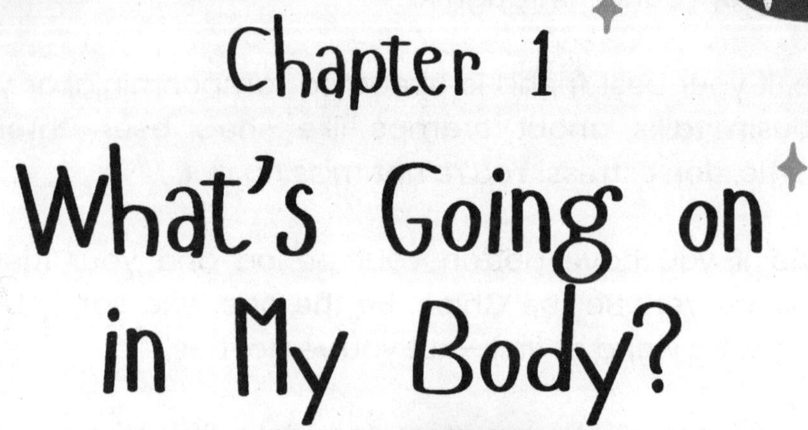

Chapter 1
What's Going on in My Body?

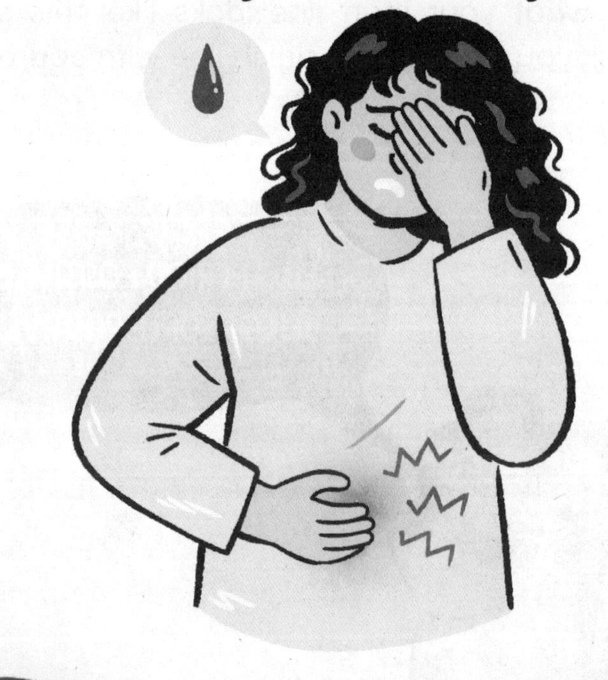

UNDERSTANDING PUBERTY

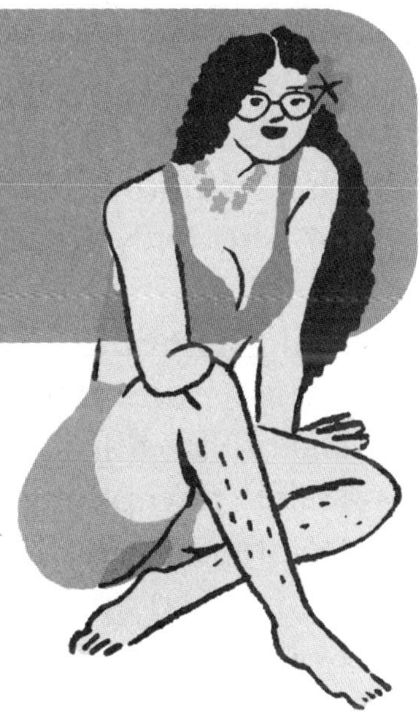

One morning, Chloe looked in the mirror and screamed.

Not because of a spider or a zit (though those are both very scream-worthy). She screamed because... her body looked *different*.

Were those hips? Was her face changing? And why were her armpits suddenly... not so fresh?

Welcome to puberty—the magical, weird, emotional rollercoaster that turns kids into teenagers and prepares your body for all kinds of adult-ish stuff (like periods, growth spurts, and feelings that sometimes come out of nowhere).

Puberty is like your body's ultimate "level up." It usually starts between ages 8 and 13, but like we said before, everyone's timeline is different. It's when your brain sends a signal to your body that says, "Hey! Time to grow!" Suddenly, things get interesting.

You might notice:

- Breast buds popping up (even if one starts before the other—totally normal!)
- Hair in new places (yes, even there)
- Height changes (hello, taller pants)
- Skin acting up (hello, pimples)
- Sweating more (welcome to deodorant life)
- Mood swings (one second you're laughing, the next you're crying over a cereal commercial)

It can be confusing, exciting, embarrassing, and empowering all at once. Chloe felt like her body had its own secret plan—and forgot to tell her about it.

But once she started learning what was actually happening, it felt way less scary and way more manageable.

Puberty also means your reproductive system is getting ready to do its thing (cue the period talk). That doesn't mean you're suddenly grown-up or need to worry about anything major—it just means your body is doing what it was designed to do.

So if you feel out of control or just plain weird sometimes, *breathe.*

You're growing. You're changing. And it's totally normal.

Chloe didn't get all the answers in one day—but with the right info and a little patience, she started to feel like her changing body was something to be proud of. And guess what? So can you.

Let's keep decoding this together.

HORMONES & BODY CHANGES

Chloe used to cry only when she got hurt—like when she once tripped over her own shoelaces at school and face-planted during gym. But lately, she noticed she could cry just because her toast fell butter-side down. Or because someone looked at her "weird." Or for no reason at all.

Spoiler: *hormones*.

Hormones are tiny chemical messengers that tell your body when and how to grow, feel, and change. During puberty, your brain (specifically the pituitary gland—yes, it's a real thing!) releases hormones that get the whole puberty party started.

The big players?

- **Estrogen** – the hormone in charge of most body changes for girls
- **Progesterone** – helps prep your body for periods
- **Growth hormone** – makes everything stretch, grow, and sometimes ache

These little messengers don't just change your body—they also impact your emotions. That's why some days you feel like dancing in your socks and other days you want to hibernate in a blanket cave forever. It's not just "moodiness." *It's biology doing its thing.*

Along with the feels, here are some body changes you might notice:

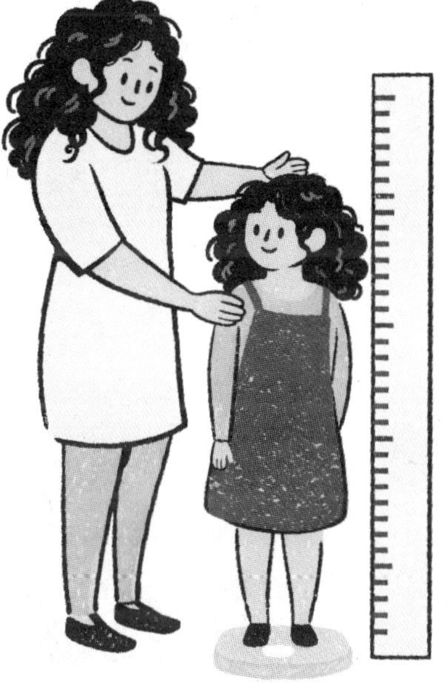

- Your chest developing (and sometimes feeling sore)
- Hair growing in places it didn't before (underarms, legs, and down below)
- Oily skin or breakouts (thanks, hormones!)
- Body odor that wasn't a thing before (deodorant = new BFF)
- A changing body shape—maybe curvier hips, a fuller belly, or more muscle

Chloe once thought her body was glitching, but really, it was just becoming her new normal. And though it felt awkward sometimes (especially when she had to buy her first bra), it also felt kind of exciting. Like she was leveling up in life.

Here's the truth: **your body is getting stronger, smarter, and more YOU every day**. That doesn't mean every moment will be perfect. But it does mean your body is working exactly the way it's supposed to.

So if you're feeling all over the place—physically or emotionally—remember that it's part of the process. And guess what? You're doing amazing.

Chloe didn't fight the changes. She learned to *roll with them*—and so will you.

BREASTS, HAIR, AND GROWTH SPURTS

One afternoon, Chloe flopped onto her bed and groaned, "Ughhh, why is one of my boobs growing faster than the other?!" She stared at her chest in the mirror, turning side to side like a detective. "Is this normal? Am I going to be lopsided forever?!"

Take a deep breath, Chloe.

And take a deep breath, you.

Because the answer is **YES**, it's normal. Totally, completely, wildly normal.

Let's talk about three big puberty moments that almost everyone wonders about (and nobody seems to explain well).

1. Breast Buds

These are usually one of the first signs that puberty has begun. They feel like little bumps under your nipples, sometimes sore or itchy. And—*surprise!*—they rarely show up perfectly at the same time. One may start growing before the other, and that's okay. They'll even out as you grow, or they'll stay a little different—and that's okay too. **Bodies aren't symmetrical.** That's completely human.

You might also start thinking about bras. A soft "training bra" or sports bra is a great starting point. Chloe felt awkward wearing one at first—until she realized almost everyone else in her class was doing the same. Now it's just part of her morning routine.

2. Hair, Hair Everywhere

Suddenly, there's hair where there used to be... well, nothing. Under your arms, on your legs, and around your vulva (that's the outside part of your private area). It can feel weird or embarrassing, especially when it first shows up.

Here's the deal: **hair is there for a reason.** It helps protect your skin and keep things comfy. Whether you shave, trim, or let it grow is your choice. There's no rulebook.

3. Growth Spurts

Have you felt like your pants turned into capris overnight? Chloe went from being one of the shortest kids in her class to almost as tall as her mom in a year. **Puberty comes with wild growth spurts where your arms, legs, and feet may grow super fast.**

You might feel clumsy (hello, spaghetti arms!) or notice stretch marks as your skin adjusts. All normal.

Chloe learned that all these changes weren't happening to her—they were happening for her. Her body was becoming stronger, taller, and more grown up, even if the process felt awkward sometimes.

So if your body feels like it's doing its own thing, don't worry. *You're not broken. You're just blooming.* And there's nothing cooler than that.

THE INSIDE STORY: UTERUS, OVARIES, AND MORE

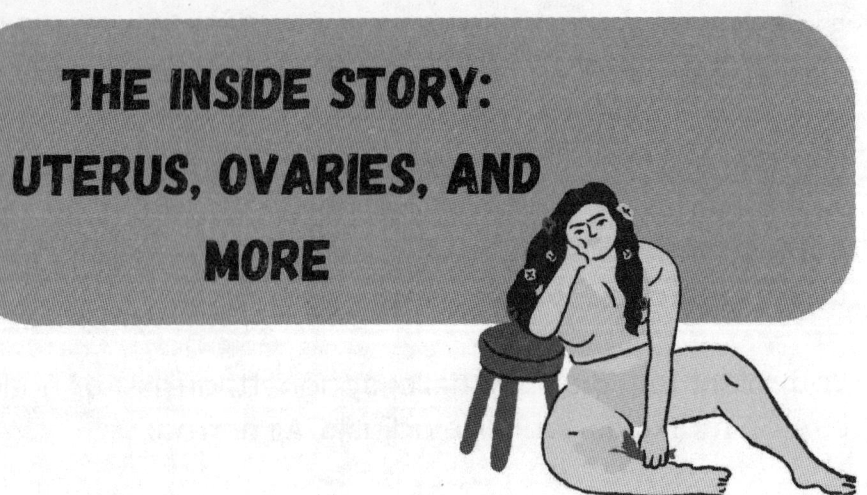

Chloe was doodling in science class when the teacher drew something totally unexpected on the board.

"It looks like... a weird upside-down squid?" she whispered to her friend. But no, it wasn't sea life. It was a diagram of the female reproductive system—aka the real MVP behind why you get periods in the first place.

Chloe used to feel a little weird thinking about all this stuff. But now? She feels empowered. Because when you understand your body, you're not just going through puberty—you're owning it.

Let's take a peek at what's happening inside your body (in a totally non-gross, super cool way). *It's time to meet Your Internal Period Team.*

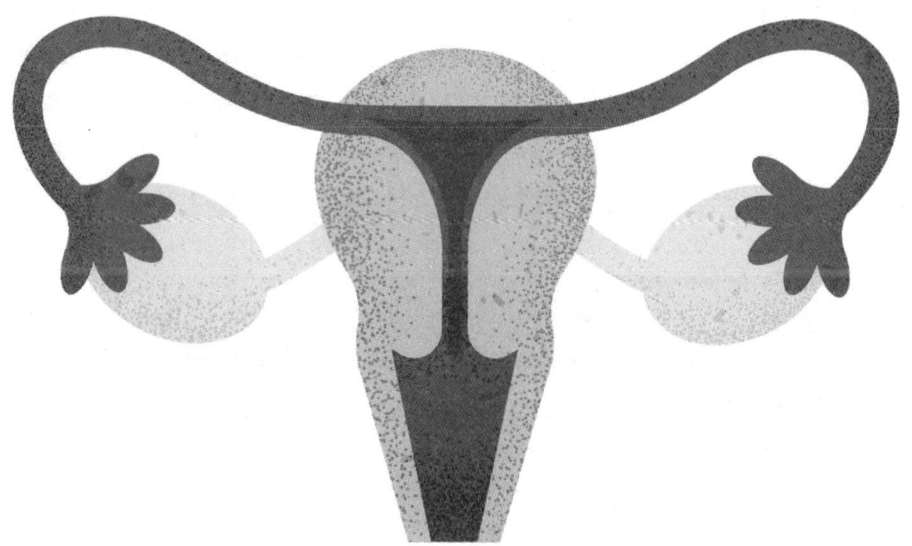

1. Uterus

This is the cozy, muscular organ where the magic happens. Every month, it builds a soft, spongy lining in case a baby were to grow there someday (don't worry, that's not happening now!). **If there's no baby, your body says, "Okay, let's clean house," and sheds the lining.** That's what you see as your period.

Chloe started calling hers "Ursula the Uterus", because if it's going to cramp, it may as well have a name.

2. Ovaries

You've got two of these, one on each side of your uterus. They're about the size of almonds and hold all the eggs you'll ever have—millions of them! **Each month, one egg (tiny, like a dot!) is released in a process called ovulation.**

3. Fallopian Tubes

These are like little bridges that connect your ovaries to your uterus. After ovulation, the egg travels through these tubes toward the uterus. It's a chill ride—unless you're in health class and everyone's giggling.

4. Cervix & Vagina

The cervix is the lower part of the uterus, like a mini doorway to the vagina, which we already learned is the stretchy canal that connects your inside world to the outside. Your period flows out through the cervix and down the vagina. Ta-da!

All these body parts are quietly doing their jobs every single month. You don't feel the egg drop or the lining build up, but trust us. *It's all happening behind the scenes like the best backstage crew ever.*

So next time someone mentions the uterus and the class snickers? You'll be the one saying, "Pfft, *amateurs*. I know all about Ursula."

Vaginas, Vulvas & How They're Different

Chloe was sitting on the edge of the bathtub, scrolling through a health app, when she gasped. "Wait... the vulva and vagina are NOT the same thing?" she whispered like she'd just uncovered a government secret. "Have I been calling everything the wrong name this whole time?!"

You're not alone, Chloe. Even adults mix up these two words. Let's clear it up, once and for all:

The Vulva

This is the outside part you can see. It includes:

- The labia (those soft skin folds)
- The clitoris (a tiny but powerful bundle of nerves)
- The urethra (where pee comes out)
- And the vaginal opening (where your period flows out and where tampons go in)

Basically, the vulva is the whole outer area of your genitals. It's kind of like the front door.

The Vagina

This is the inside tunnel that connects the vaginal opening to the uterus. You can't see it by looking in a mirror—it's internal. It's stretchy, strong, and amazing. This is where menstrual blood flows from, and where a tampon (if you use one) would go. You can think of it as the hallway inside the house.

So, Chloe wasn't "wrong" for saying vagina before—it's just that now she knows there's more to the story. And once you understand your body better, you start feeling way more in control of what's going on.

And guess what? You don't need to be shy or embarrassed about these words. They're just body parts—like elbows and knees, only way more underappreciated.

Let's also get one thing straight: ***your vulva is normal***. Whether it's small, big, darker, lighter, smooth, or hairy—it's normal. Chloe used to worry hers looked "weird" until she learned there's no such thing as a "perfect" vulva. Everyone's is different, and that's awesome.

So if you've ever wondered what's really going on down there, now you know:

- *Vulva = outside*
- *Vagina = inside*

Knowing your body is power. And now, you're officially smarter than most grown-ups. Go, you!

WORD SEARCH

Find the words listed below and circle them.

A	G	P	U	B	E	R	T	Y	X	U	C
H	E	R	T	U	H	J	K	L	D	T	S
O	S	O	O	L	C	F	R	X	L	E	J
R	T	R	F	W	B	Y	D	W	S	R	O
M	R	S	H	F	T	M	C	L	K	U	U
O	O	F	G	K	Y	H	S	L	W	S	B
N	G	P	I	M	P	L	E	T	E	N	M
E	E	R	O	V	A	R	I	E	S	H	D
T	N	M	O	O	D	I	O	D	S	K	L

- PUBERTY
- HORMONE
- ESTROGEN
- GROWTH
- PIMPLE
- MOOD
- UTERUS
- OVARIES
- CYCLE

TRUE OR FALSE?

Tick the correct answer.

Statement	True	False
Everyone starts puberty at the same age.	○	○
Getting taller quickly is called a growth spurt.	○	○
Puberty only affects girls.	○	○
Hormones help tell your body when to grow and change.	○	○
Puberty only affects how your body looks.	○	○

Chapter 2
What Is a
Period, Anyway?

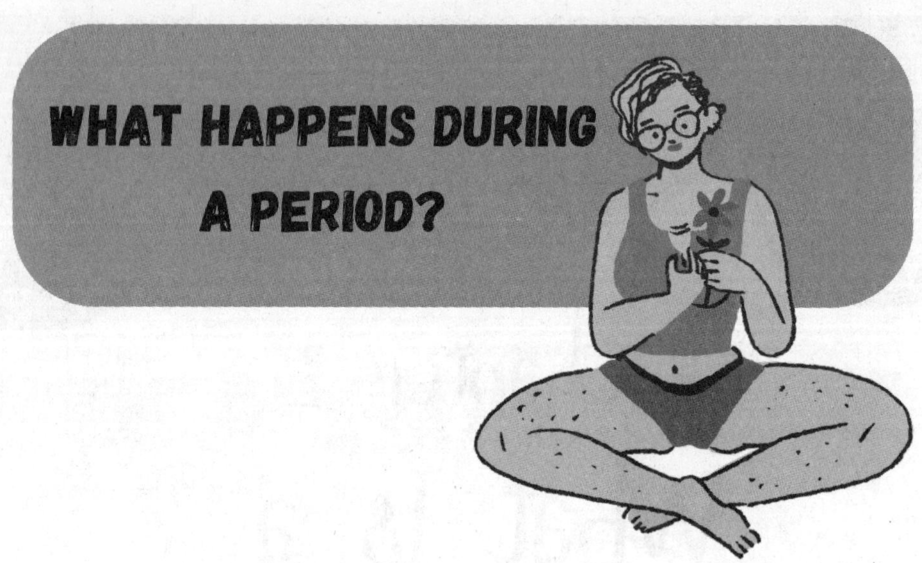

WHAT HAPPENS DURING A PERIOD?

When Chloe got her first period, she thought something was seriously wrong. She was at her cousin's house, watching a movie, when she went to the bathroom and saw blood. Not a little dot—like, actual blood. Her stomach flipped. "Do I need a doctor? Is this an emergency?!"

Nope. It was just her uterus doing its monthly thing.

So... what is a period, really?

Let's break it down like this:

Your uterus is a little overachiever. Every month, it builds up a soft, squishy lining full of blood and nutrients—just in case a baby were ever to grow there one day. (Reminder: this doesn't mean you're having a baby, like, ever soon.)

When no baby shows up (which is almost always the case for teens), your body says, "Cool, let's clean this up," and sheds that lining. The result? A period —aka the release of that lining through the vagina.

Here's what you might notice:

- Blood (light to heavier red, sometimes brownish)
- Some clumps or goo (totally normal—those are bits of the lining!)
- Flow that lasts 3 to 7 days
- A pattern that repeats every 28-ish days (but it's different for everyone)

The first few periods can be all over the place. Chloe's first one lasted 2 days, then nothing for 3 months. It's normal for it to be unpredictable at first. Your body's just learning its rhythm.

You might also feel things like:

- Cramping (like a tummy ache but lower down)
- Back aches
- Feeling more tired or cranky
- Wanting to hug a giant stuffed animal and eat chocolate (100% relatable)

Is it fun? Not really. But is it manageable? Totally.

In short:

- **No baby = uterus sheds its lining**
- **The lining = what becomes your period**

The blood you see isn't a wound or an injury. You're not losing something important.

In fact, your body quickly makes up for it, and the cycle starts again.

And why does it happen every month? Because your body is super organized. It's on a schedule. Chloe once joked that her uterus had a calendar app. "Next period: 26 days. Reminder: buy chocolate."

Here's the cool part: **this cycle is ancient. Like, as old as humanity.** Every person with a uterus has gone through it, from ancient queens to astronauts in space. Yes—there are literally astronauts floating in zero gravity who've managed periods just fine. If they can do it, so can you.

When Chloe first learned she'd be bleeding every month, her exact words were: "Wait. I lose blood. Every month. And I'm still expected to do math homework?"

Totally fair reaction. But once she understood why this was happening, it started to feel less terrifying and way more... awesome. Because **bleeding is actually one of the coolest signs that your body is working exactly right**.

Chloe learned to track her period so she wouldn't get caught off guard. She started carrying a mini emergency kit with pads and extra underwear—just in case. And soon, her period became less of a "AHHHH!" and more of a "Oh, right. *You* again."

And now that you know what's happening, you're already way ahead of where Chloe was on day one.

THE MENSTRUAL CYCLE TIMELINE

Chloe was staring at her planner one night, trying to figure out why she was feeling moody, bloated, and like she could cry over a dropped cookie. "What is going on with me?" she groaned, hugging a heat pack like it was her emotional support pet.

Turns out... it was day 25 of her menstrual cycle.

Understanding your menstrual cycle is like unlocking the secret code behind your body's behaviors. It's not just "you bleed, then it stops." **There's a whole flow (pun intended) happening inside you every single month**.

Once Chloe understood this rhythm, she started tracking her cycle on a free app. Suddenly, everything made more sense. No more surprises, fewer freak-outs, and way more confidence.

MENSTRUAL CYCLE

Menstrual
(Day 1-7)

REST
& REFLECT

Focus:
Letting go, clarity

Follicular
(Day 8-14)

CREATE
& PLAN

Focus:
New ideas, playfulness

Ovulation
(Day 15-21)

SHARE
& CONNECT

Focus:
Visibility, expression

Luteal
(Day 22-28)

SLOW DOWN
& INTEGRATE

Focus:
Completion, self-care

Here's a simple breakdown of the four main phases.

1. Menstrual Phase (Days 1–5-ish):
This is when your period happens. Your uterus is shedding its lining (the one it made just in case of pregnancy), and blood flows out through the vagina. You might feel tired, crampy, or snack-obsessed. That's totally normal.

Chloe's tip: comfy pants + chocolate = survival mode.

2. Follicular Phase (Days 1–13):
This phase starts at the same time as your period. Your brain signals your ovaries to get a few eggs ready. One follicle (a tiny bubble holding an egg) gets chosen as the "star" egg for this cycle. Meanwhile, your uterus starts building a brand-new lining.

You may start to feel more energetic and focused as this phase moves along.

3. Ovulation (~Day 14):
The chosen egg is released from the ovary and travels down the fallopian tube. This is called ovulation. If it meets a sperm, pregnancy could happen—but for most teens, that's not happening. The egg just dissolves later.

Some people feel a little twinge or cramp during ovulation—called *mittelschmerz* (fancy German word alert!).

4. Luteal Phase (Days 15–28):
Your body waits to see if the egg is fertilized. Spoiler: usually not. So hormone levels start dropping, which causes PMS symptoms like mood swings, bloating, or crying over commercials about puppies.

Then—BOOM—it's period time again, and the cycle repeats.

Your body runs on a schedule. *Now that you know it, you're in sync with it.* That's some next-level grown-up energy right there.

Period Myths Debunked

When Chloe got her first period, her cousin whispered, "You can't shower now, you know. The water might stop your flow and mess up your cycle!"

Chloe blinked. "Wait... I can't SHOWER?!"

Spoiler: *you definitely can. And should.*

There are so many wild myths about periods floating around—some are ancient, some are just silly, and a few are downright confusing. But don't worry, we're about to bust them like period detectives.

MYTH #1: You can't shower on your period.

Totally false. Taking a warm shower can actually help with cramps and make you feel clean and fresh. Chloe loves using a lavender body wash and singing at full volume—it's part of her "period care ritual."

MYTH #2: You can't swim during your period.

As long as you use a tampon or menstrual cup, you can absolutely swim. Your flow won't magically turn the pool red. Chloe wore a dark swimsuit and swam with her friends like nothing was different.

MYTH #3: Period blood is dirty.

I mean, it's just blood inside the uterus. Completely natural, not gross or toxic. In fact, your period is your body's way of staying healthy.

MYTH #4: Everyone will be able to tell.

Not true. Unless you walk around announcing it with a megaphone, no one can tell you have your period. If you're worried about leaks, wear a pad with wings or bring extras in your bag.

MYTH #5: You can't play sports or dance.

So false. You can do everything you usually do—run, jump, cartwheel, TikTok dance battle—on your period. If anything, movement helps reduce cramps and boost your mood.

There are even myths in some cultures that say girls shouldn't touch plants, cook, or go near animals during their periods. *Major eye roll.* Those ideas come from a long history of not understanding how the body works. But YOU? You're not falling for any of that. You've got the facts. So the next time someone whispers something suspicious about your cycle, you can smile and say, "Actually... I know what's really going on."

WORD SEARCH

Find the words listed below and circle them.

O	R	C	L	O	T	Y	U	F	G	N	L
T	V	P	E	R	I	O	D	M	Q	L	I
Q	V	U	Y	R	D	S	O	F	E	Z	N
U	E	G	L	S	V	B	L	L	J	S	I
L	U	T	E	A	L	I	W	O	Y	M	N
W	L	R	G	I	T	S	X	W	E	G	G
F	G	I	J	L	W	I	G	S	D	P	F
L	N	I	D	W	H	U	O	U	I	O	U
A	U	G	F	H	F	K	J	N	O	Y	W

- OVULATION
- VAGINA
- PERIOD
- CERVIX
- EGG
- LUTEAL
- LINING
- CLOT
- FLOW

CREATE YOUR OWN

COMIC STRIP

Draw the story of what happens inside your body each month.

Chapter 3

First Period Feelings

FIRST PERIOD FEELINGS

When Chloe got her first period, she didn't cry. She didn't scream. She didn't even faint (though she thought she might). She just sat on the toilet and stared at her underwear like it had betrayed her.

Then the emotions came in waves.

- **Confusion**: "Is this really it?"
- **Panic**: "Do I even have pads??"
- **Embarrassment**: "Should I tell Mom?"
- **Curiosity**: "Is it supposed to look like that?"
- **Pride**: "Wait... does this mean I'm growing up?"

First periods are not one-size-fits-all. For some people, it's a quiet, chill "oh, cool" moment. For others, it's a total drama episode, complete with tears, texts to best friends, and a dramatic sigh into a pillow.

Chloe landed somewhere in the middle—equal parts proud and confused.

And you know what? Every reaction is okay.

It's totally normal to feel:

- Nervous or weird
- Embarrassed (even though you shouldn't be)
- Giddy and grown-up
- Overwhelmed by the responsibility of it all
- A mix of everything, all at once

Some people even feel horribly sad during their first few cycles. That doesn't mean you're doing anything wrong. **Hormones can mess with emotions big time—especially at the start.**

So if you find yourself tearing up at cat videos or snapping at your brother for chewing too loud, *welcome to the club.* Chloe once cried because she couldn't decide between two snack options. (She chose both.)

Here's the truth: **a first period is a huge moment, even if no one around you makes a big deal of it.** Your body just did something incredible. It flipped a switch and said, "We're ready now." That deserves a little celebration—even if it's just a chocolate bar and a moment of "Wow, I did it."

And hey, if you feel a little awkward, that's cool too. Chloe didn't tell anyone for two days. Then she finally whispered it to her mom while pretending to look for her charger. Her mom hugged her and said, "I'm so proud of you." Chloe cried again—this time, happy tears.

So if your feelings are all over the place right now? Good. That means you're exactly where you're supposed to be.

WHAT IF IT'S EARLY? WHAT IF IT'S LATE?

Chloe was 12 and still period-less. Her friends had started whispering in the bathroom, sharing pad recommendations and cramp horror stories. Chloe laughed along—but inside, she was wondering, When is it going to be MY turn?

Meanwhile, her cousin Mia got her first period at just 9. "I didn't even know what a uterus was yet," Mia once said, rolling her eyes. "I thought I was dying!"

So... who's normal?

Both of them.

Here's the truth: **there's no perfect age to start your period.** It usually happens between ages 9 and 14, but some start earlier or later, and it's all totally okay.

What if your period comes early?

You might be the first in your friend group. That can feel weird or even isolating. Mia felt embarrassed until she realized that being "first" didn't mean she was weird—it just meant her body was ready sooner.

If that's you, know this: *you are not alone, and your body is just ahead of the curve.*

What if your period comes late?

Chloe was convinced something was wrong. Everyone around her seemed to have theirs already. She even googled, "Am I broken if I don't have my period yet?" (Spoiler: she wasn't.)

Some bodies take a little longer. Maybe your hormones are still warming up. As long as you're showing other signs of puberty—like breast development or pubic hair—your period is on its way.

If you're 15 or older with zero signs of puberty, that's a good time to check in with a doctor. If not? Deep breath. You're right on time for you.

WORD SEARCH

Find the words listed below and circle them.

S	U	P	P	O	R	T	V	Y	N	S	U
C	O	N	F	U	S	E	D	R	F	G	N
A	C	H	A	N	G	E	G	B	S	C	C
R	O	F	H	E	N	M	A	T	Q	P	E
E	M	B	A	R	R	A	S	S	E	D	R
D	F	Z	F	G	T	E	M	H	Y	A	T
C	O	U	R	A	G	E	Y	U	P	S	A
G	R	E	L	I	E	V	E	D	S	D	I
O	T	G	L	W	N	M	S	Y	U	P	N

- CONFUSED
- EMBARRASSED
- CHANGE
- RELIEVED
- COMFORT
- COURAGE
- SCARED
- SUPPORT
- UNCERTAIN

FEELINGS JAR

Check-in with your own feelings and fill this container with feeling colors to show how much of each you have

Angry (Red)	Happy (Yellow)	Sad (Blue)
Nervous (Purple)	Excited (Green)	Calm (Orange)

Chapter 4
All About Period Products

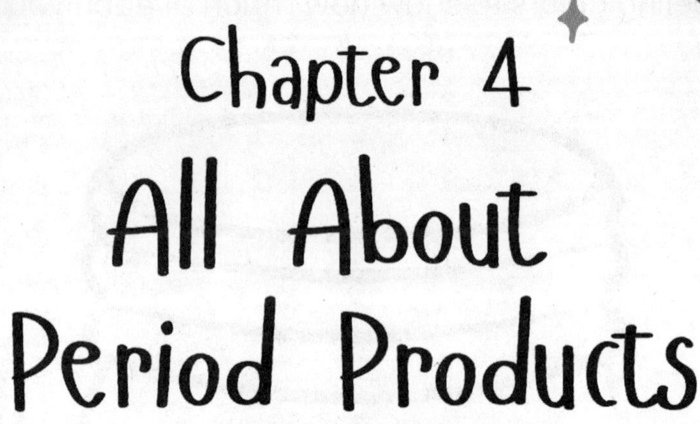

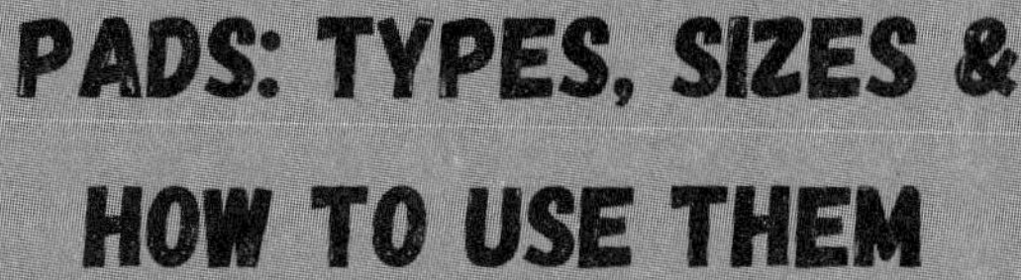

Chloe's first experience with a pad was... let's just say, confusing. She opened the wrapper like it was a mystery snack, stared at the sticky side, and asked, "Wait... does this go in my underwear or... on me?"

Totally normal reaction.

So let's break down the basics of pads, a.k.a. the easiest and most common period product to start with.

What is a pad?

A pad is a soft, absorbent strip that sticks to the inside of your underwear. Its job? To catch your period flow and keep you comfy and dry. Unlike tampons or menstrual cups, *pads stay outside your body*—no inserting required.

Chloe found that comforting at first. "It's like a secret cushion for your undies," she said. (Kind of accurate.)

Types of Pads:

- **Regular pads:** great for medium flow days
- **Thin/pantyliners:** for very light days or just spotting
- **Super/overnight pads:** thicker and longer—perfect for heavier flow or nighttime
- **Pads with wings:** have sticky flaps that wrap around the sides of your underwear to keep the pad in place (Chloe's personal fav)

There are also pads made from organic cotton, scented ones (not always the best for sensitive skin), and reusable cloth options if you want to be eco-friendly.

How to Use a Pad:

1. **Unwrap the pad:** some even make fun crinkly noises like chip bags (just roll with it).
2. **Stick the adhesive side onto the inside of your underwear**, lengthwise. If it has wings, wrap those around the sides.
3. **Pull up your underwear**, adjust, and boom—you're ready to roll.

Pro Tip:
Keep some "period underwear" in a size smaller than your usual size. This ensures your pads stay nice and snug, preventing that annoying flag of Japan on your bed.

How often should you change it?

Every 4–6 hours, or sooner if it feels full or starts to smell. Chloe sets reminders on her phone, especially during school days.

Always wrap used pads in toilet paper or the wrapper and toss them in the bin—not the toilet. **Pads and plumbing are NOT friends.**

Chloe's first pad felt like wearing a mattress between her legs, but after a few days, she forgot it was even there. With a little trial and error, you'll figure out what works best for you.

Pads = period superheroes.

And now you know exactly how to use them.

TAMPONS: WHAT TO KNOW BEFORE TRYING

Chloe was at the pool with her friends when disaster struck—her period showed up, totally uninvited.

"Can't I just swim with a pad?" she whispered to her friend, panicking.

Her friend shook her head. "Time to meet... the tampon."

Chloe's eyes widened. "You mean the thing that goes *inside*?!"

Yes. That thing.

And yes, it sounds a little intimidating at first. But once you understand how tampons work, they become just another option in your period toolkit.

What is a tampon?

A tampon is a small, absorbent cylinder made of soft cotton that you insert into your vagina (remember, that's the inside tunnel, not the outside). It soaks up your period from the inside and expands as it absorbs.

It sounds wild, but it's safe, it doesn't hurt if inserted correctly, and it gives you more freedom to swim, dance, or wear leggings without the "diaper" feeling.

Tampon Truths:

- They don't get "lost" inside you. Your vagina has a definite end (your cervix), so the tampon stays put until you remove it.
- There's a string. It hangs out so you can pull the tampon out easily.
- It doesn't mean anything about your "virginity." Using a tampon is just easy period care.

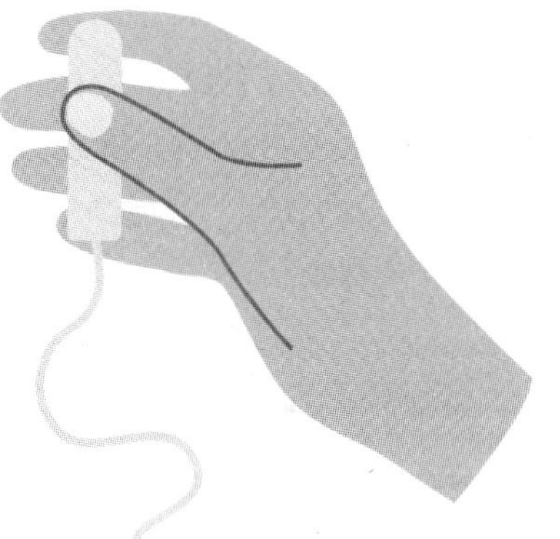

It might feel weird the first few times. That's normal! Chloe tried three times before she got it right—and did a happy dance when it finally felt comfortable.

How to Use a Tampon (Starter Version):

- Wash your hands. Always.
- Get into a comfy position. Standing with one foot on the toilet or sitting is great.
- Hold the tampon with the applicator. Gently insert it into your vagina until your fingers touch your body.
- Push the smaller tube (the plunger) into the larger one. This slides the tampon in.
- Remove the applicator. Just the string stays out.
- You're done!

Change every 4–6 hours. *Never wear one longer than 8 hours* (to avoid TSS, a super rare but serious condition).

Chloe once thought she'd never use tampons. Now? She keeps a few in her pool bag—just in case. *Tampons aren't scary when you know the facts.* And now, you totally do.

PERIOD UNDERWEAR & MENSTRUAL CUPS

Chloe was scrolling through her favorite online shop when she saw something labeled "leak-proof period underwear."

She squinted at the screen. "Wait... underwear that absorbs BLOOD?!"

Yep.

Welcome to the magical world of period underwear and menstrual cups. These are two of the coolest, eco-friendliest, and sometimes *weirdest-sounding* period products out there.

But don't worry, we're here to decode them both.

Period Underwear

Think of it like regular undies, but with superpowers. These high-tech panties are designed with layers that absorb period blood without leaking, feeling wet, or making you feel like you're wearing a diaper.

Chloe tried them on a chill weekend at home and was like, "Okay... why didn't anyone tell me this existed?!"

Here's why they're awesome:

- They're versatile! You can wear them on light days, as backup with a tampon, or even overnight.
- They come in all sizes, styles, and colors (yup, even cute ones).
- You just wash and reuse them—no pads needed!

Downsides?

They can be a little pricey, and you'll need a few pairs to rotate while the others are in the wash.

It might feel weird the first few times. That's normal! Chloe tried three times before she got it right—and did a happy dance when it finally felt comfortable.

Menstrual Cups

Okay, now this one sounds wild, but stick with us.

A menstrual cup is a *soft, bendable cup* (usually made of silicone) that you fold and insert into your vagina. It opens up, catches your period inside. You empty it every 8–12 hours, rinse, reinsert, and boom—you're good to go.

Why some people love cups:

- One cup can last YEARS (seriously, it's that eco-friendly).
- You don't feel it once it's in right.
- It holds way more than a tampon

BUT:

- It takes practice to get in and out.
- You've got to be okay with seeing blood when emptying it.

So which one's best?

Answer: whatever works for YOU.

Chloe's still experimenting. Some days she's a pad person. Some days, she rocks her leak-proof shorts.

You don't have to pick one forever. **Period care = choose your own adventure.**

How to Choose What's Right for You

Chloe stood in the period product aisle at the store, eyes wide.

Pads, tampons, liners, cups, underwear... "Why are there SO MANY OPTIONS?" she muttered. "Is there a starter kit or something?!"

Truth is, *there's no one-size-fits-all when it comes to period products*. Your flow, comfort, activity level, and even mood can change what you want to use.

But don't panic—we're here to help you figure out what works best for you.

Let's play Period Matchmaker!

If you're brand new to periods and want to keep it simple:

Try: Pads

They're easy to use, stay outside the body, and come in lots of shapes and sizes. Chloe started with pads and felt secure knowing she could just stick, adjust, and go.

If you want to move around a lot or swim:

Try: Tampons or Menstrual Cups

Tampons are great for activities and swimming—once you get the hang of inserting them. Cups are amazing if you're up for trying something reusable and long-wear.

If you have heavy flow days:

Try: Super pads or tampons with backup

A combo like a tampon + pantyliner or a menstrual cup + period underwear can help you feel covered, just in case your flow is heavier.

Still not sure?

Mix it up!

Chloe carries pads in her backpack, uses period underwear at home, and is slowly building courage to try tampons. Most people switch based on the day, their flow, or how they're feeling.

What matters is that you feel safe, comfy, and confident. If something feels off—leaky, itchy, or just not "you"—try something different.

Chloe used to feel overwhelmed by all the options. Now? She's building her own "period kit" like a boss.

And you will too.

WORD SEARCH

Find the words listed below and circle them.

G	A	U	L	F	K	W	U	X	M	U	U
A	P	P	L	I	C	A	T	O	R	N	F
G	H	R	P	W	G	N	U	A	D	H	Y
S	F	Y	A	H	Y	S	B	E	Q	M	L
Y	E	L	D	I	S	C	R	E	E	T	I
C	U	P	S	T	J	W	I	P	E	S	W
J	L	G	K	R	E	U	S	E	A	N	P
N	P	W	U	A	T	A	M	P	O	N	S
E	J	F	R	E	S	H	Q	H	U	R	N

- PADS
- TAMPONS
- CUPS
- DISCREET
- UNDERWEAR
- WIPES
- APPLICATOR
- FRESH
- REUSE

COMFORT CHECK

Rate how comfortable each product seems to you.

PADS

TAMPONS

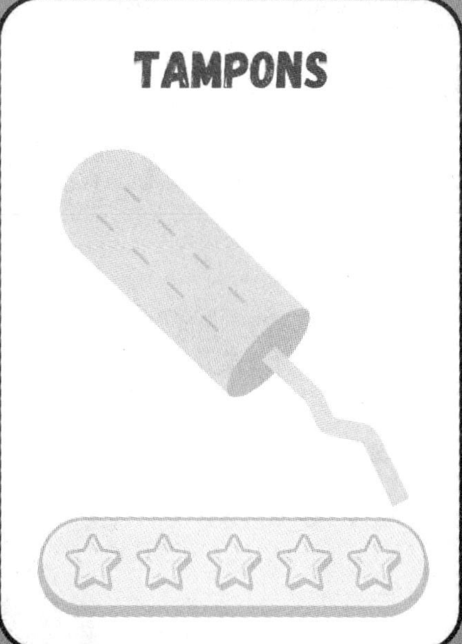

MENSTRUAL CUPS

PERIOD UNDERWEAR

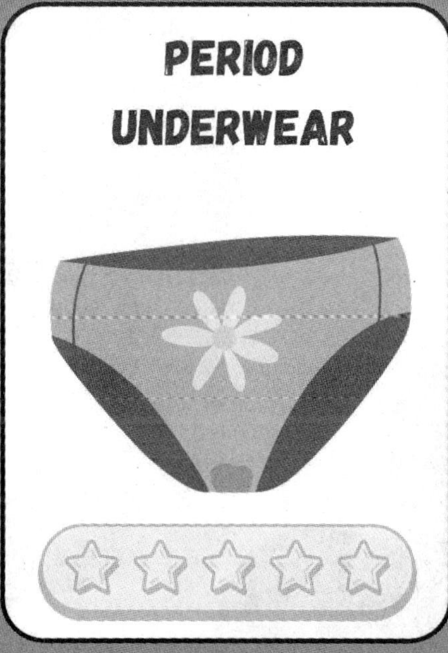

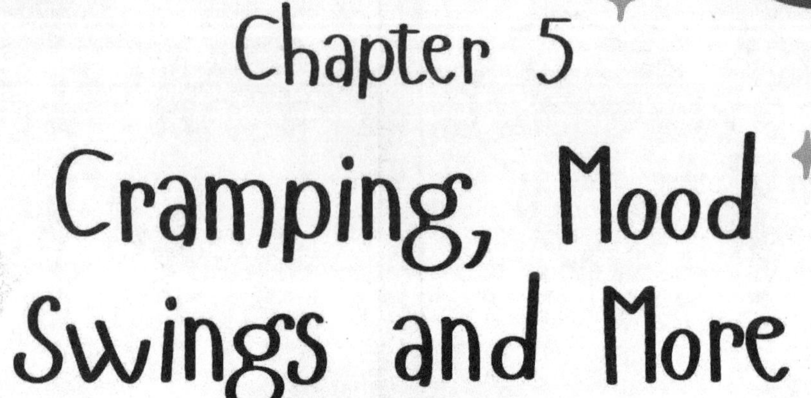

Chapter 5

Cramping, Mood Swings and More

WHY CRAMPS?

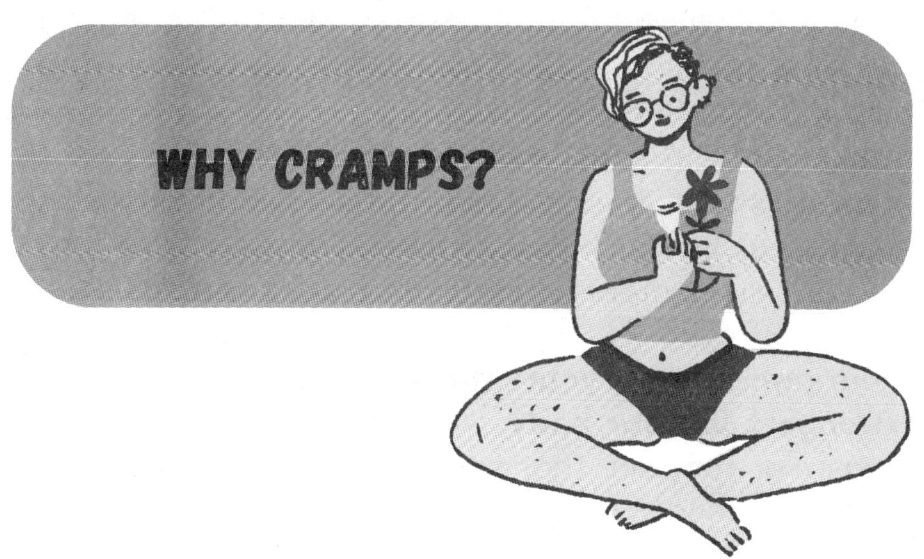

Chloe was lying on her bed, curled up like a cinnamon roll. “Ow, ow, OW,” she muttered. “What is my uterus doing, fighting crime?”

Nope—it was just cramps, the not-so-fun sidekick to periods. Some months, it’s like your uterus goes full drama queen.

Chloe learned this the hard way during her second period, when she had to cancel a movie night because of the pain. She thought something was wrong. Turns out, it was just her body working like normal.

The good news? **Cramps are common and totally manageable.** You’re not broken. You’re just having a moment with your body’s natural rhythm. And soon, you’ll know exactly how to handle it like the boss you are.

So... why do cramps happen?

Chloe once asked her science teacher, "If cramps are so normal, why do they feel like I'm being karate-chopped from the inside?" Her teacher laughed and said, "Because your uterus is literally flexing its muscles."

Here's what's wild: **your uterus is a muscle—one of the strongest in your body.** And like any muscle, it can spasm or contract. That's its way of pushing out what it no longer needs.

Each month, your uterus builds a lining to prepare for a possible pregnancy. When there's no pregnancy, your body has to shed that lining. To do this, your uterus contracts—literally squeezes—to push out the extra tissue and blood.

These squeezes? That's what you feel as cramps.

Those contractions are triggered by chemicals called **prostaglandins**. The more prostaglandins your body releases, the stronger the cramps can feel.

These contractions are usually strongest on the first couple days of your period, when your flow is heaviest.

You might feel:

- A dull ache in your lower belly
- Sharp twinges that come and go
- Pain in your back or thighs (yep, that's connected too)
- A heavy, bloated feeling

Cramps are different for everyone. Chloe's were mild at first, then got stronger the next cycle. Her friend Layla barely gets cramps at all (lucky). Some people have intense cramps called dysmenorrhea, and that may need a doctor's help.

The key is knowing your body. And don't worry, we'll get to all the ways to soothe them in just a couple pages. But first, let's look at what can make cramps worse—or better.

Some days, Chloe's cramps felt like background noise—annoying but manageable. Other days, they took over her whole mood. That's because **certain things can make cramps worse**... and some can help keep them chill.

Here's what might make cramps feel more intense:

- Too many prostaglandins: Your body naturally produces these chemicals, but some people make more than others. More prostaglandins = stronger cramps.
- Stress: If you're anxious or tense, your body holds onto pain more. That's why a calm mind helps!
- Not moving enough: Weird, right? But lying in bed all day can make cramps worse. Gentle movement actually helps loosen things up.
- Caffeine overload: That iced coffee or chocolate bar might feel comforting, but caffeine tightens blood vessels, which can make cramps worse.

And here's what can ease the cramping:

- Warmth (hello, heating pad!)
- Movement (like stretching)
- Exercise (whatever you can)
- Drinking water
- Deep breathing
- Resting in a cozy, curled-up position

Chloe started keeping a "cramp kit" in her room: heating pad, socks, a water bottle, and her favorite comfort shows. Total game changer. She felt less like a victim of her body and more like a girl who *just gets it.*

The key takeaway?

Cramps = normal.

Pain that stops you from doing daily stuff = talk to an adult.

Most cramps can be managed with smart choices. But if your cramps are:

- So strong you miss school
- Making you throw up
- Lasting longer than your period
- Getting worse every cycle

...then it's time to check in with a doctor. Some girls experience conditions like **endometriosis** or **PMDD**, and those need real medical care—not just chocolate and Netflix.

Chloe keeps track of her symptoms now. Because knowing why cramps happen gives you something super powerful: control.

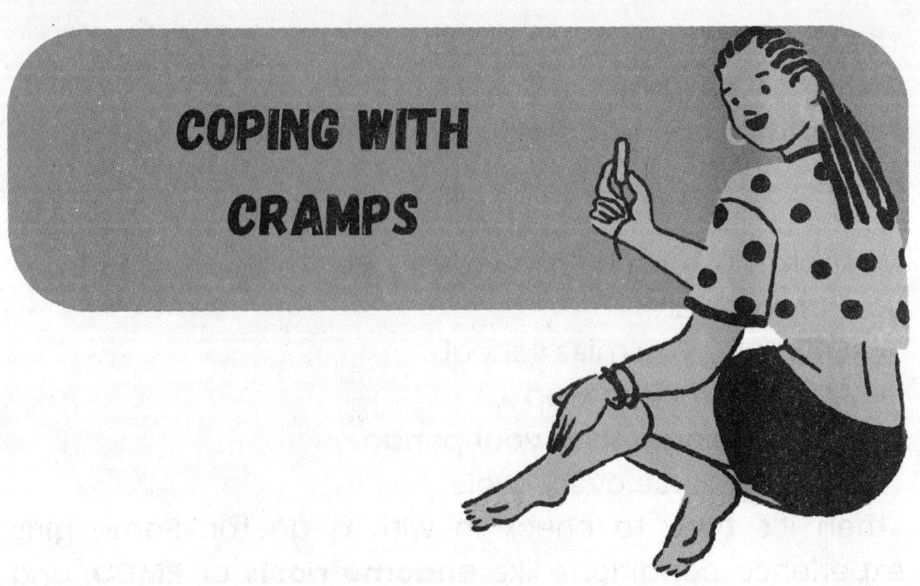

COPING WITH CRAMPS

Chloe woke up one Saturday feeling like a crab had pinched her lower belly and refused to let go.

"Ugh, not again," she groaned, clutching her stomach. But this time, she was ready.

She reached for her heating pad, wrapped herself in a fuzzy blanket, and flipped on her favorite comfort show.

Within minutes, the pain was softer. Less shouty. More like a whisper.

Welcome to your cramp-soothing tool kit: *a list of things that can turn "owww" into "I've got this."*

Let's start with the MVP: **heat**.

Applying warmth to your lower belly helps relax the muscles of your uterus and calms those contractions. It's basically like telling your uterus, "Shhh. You're okay."

Ways to use heat:

- Heating pad: Electric or microwavable—Chloe's is shaped like a unicorn.
- Warm water bottle: Wrapped in a towel, it does the trick.
- Warm bath: Bonus points if it includes bubbles and a good playlist.
- Warmth-on-the-go: Stick-on heat patches you can wear under your clothes at school or while traveling.

Heat isn't magic—but it sure feels like it when your cramps start melting away.

Once Chloe had heat on her side, she started experimenting with other cramp-busting tricks. "Okay, if my uterus is going to act dramatic, I'm going to fight back—with kindness."
Here are some of her go-to remedies that actually help:

1. Gentle Movement
When you're cramping, lying down forever seems like a good idea, but moving actually helps. Gentle stretches, light yoga, or even walking around your room can loosen your muscles and release feel-good chemicals called endorphins. *Some of these can even be done lying down!*

Chloe started doing five-minute yoga videos in her room. "Crampy girl stretches" became her thing.

2. Hydration
Drinking water helps your body stay balanced. When you're dehydrated, cramps can feel worse. *Aim for warm water or herbal teas.* Peppermint and chamomile are especially soothing.

3. Pain Relief (if you need it)
If cramps are too strong, it's okay to use an over-the-counter pain reliever—but only with an adult's permission. *Meds like ibuprofen or naproxen* help reduce inflammation, which eases cramps fast.

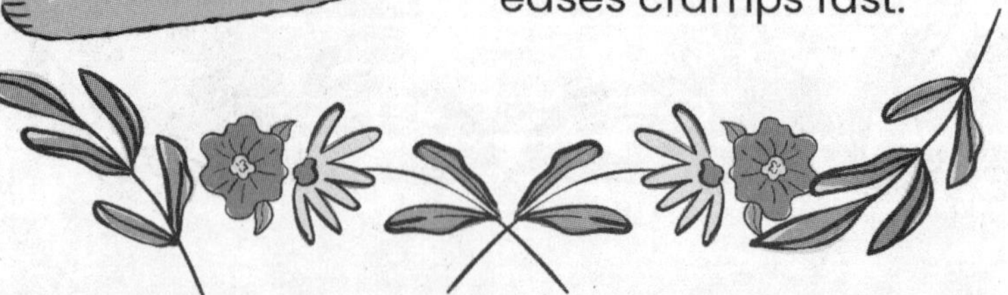

Some people think you have to "tough it out" through cramps, but Chloe knows better now—comfort is self-care, not weakness.

It wasn't about pretending the pain didn't exist. It was about saying, "I hear you. Let's make this easier together."

She packed a mini version of her kit for school:

- A stick-on heat patch
- A little roll-on essential oil (lavender or peppermint)
- A snack (dark chocolate, yes please)
- A water bottle
- A period pouch with pads and spare underwear

Cramp days were still crampy... but they didn't control her life anymore.

You don't have to suffer through your period. You can respond to it. And the more you listen to what makes you feel better, the more in control you'll feel every cycle.

Cramps may be part of the period package, but here's what Chloe finally realized they didn't have to take over her life. Some months, they're mild. Other months, they hit harder. But every time, she's a little more prepared. **She treats her body like a friend, not an enemy.**

Most importantly, remember: you are not weak for feeling pain. You are not dramatic. You're just experiencing something completely natural, and it's okay to need rest, support, *and* chocolate.

Chloe used to dread her cramps. Now she sees them as a signal to slow down and care for herself.

You've got everything you need to handle this. *When you're gentle with yourself, cramps become way more manageable.*

Next up? All those feelings that come with your period. Let's talk about mood swings.

Cramp Survival Checklist

- [ ] Heat: pad or stick-on patch
- [ ] Movement: Stretch, walk, or do yoga
- [ ] Hydration: water > soda!
- [ ] The ultimate: warm water!
- [ ] Avoid: caffeine or salt
- [ ] Don't forget: breathe!

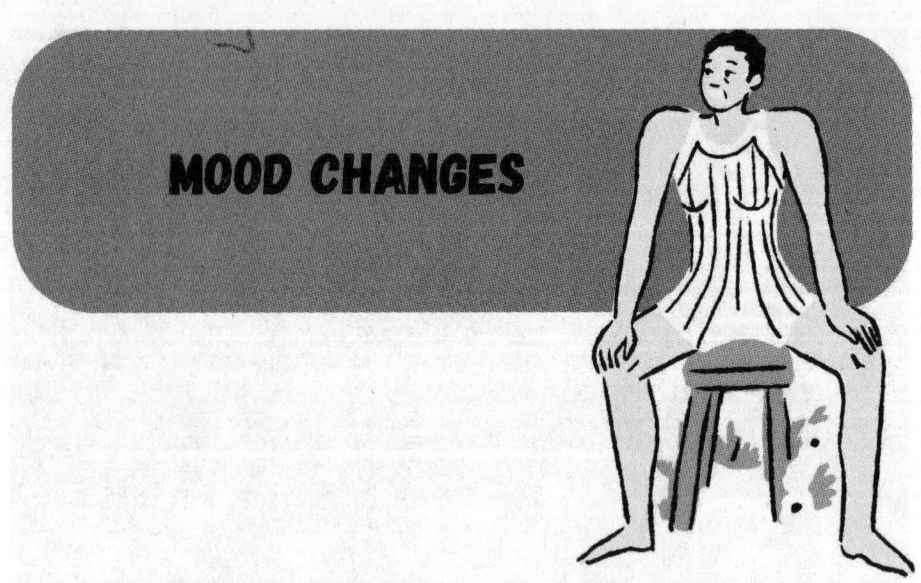

MOOD CHANGES

Chloe was halfway through math homework when she burst into tears.

Why? Because she couldn't find the right pencil.

That's it. The *pencil.*

Five minutes later, she was laughing at a dog meme. Then grumpy. Then sleepy. Then crying again—this time because her cereal got soggy.

If that sounds familiar, welcome to the wild world of period emotions.

Mood swings aren't all in your head. They're very real, and they happen because of... you guessed it: **hormones**.

Right before and during your period, **your estrogen and progesterone levels drop.** These hormones don't just affect your body—they affect your brain. The result? Emotions that feel louder, heavier, or just... weird.

Chloe calls it her "emotional tornado week."

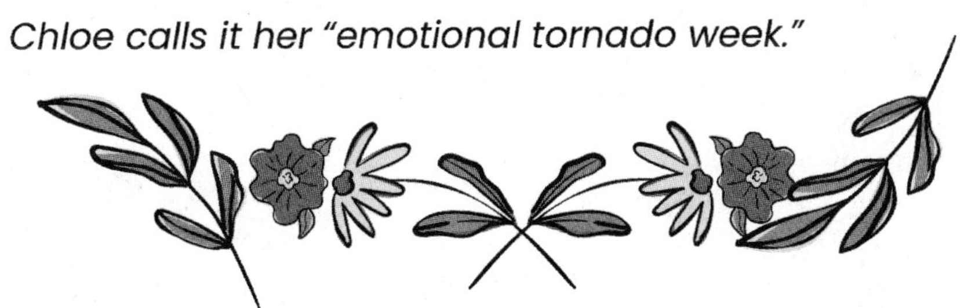

Chloe used to think her moods made her "too much." Too dramatic. Too sensitive. Too grumpy. But after learning about hormones, she realized it wasn't about being too anything—it was about learning how to ride the wave, not fight it.

So, how do you deal when your feelings feel bigger than your backpack?

1. Name It to Tame It

Instead of saying "I'm losing it," try:
"I'm feeling extra irritable today. Maybe it's PMS."
Giving your feelings a name makes them feel less out of control. Especially when you know what causes it.

2. Journal or Doodle It Out

Chloe started writing her feelings in a journal, just a few lines a day. Some days she drew a grumpy cloud. Some days, a dancing banana. *Whatever helped her process.*

***3.* Let Yourself Cry**

Yep. Crying is not weakness. It's your body's way of saying, "I've got a lot inside, and I need to let it out." Chloe used to cry in her blanket fort. It helped.

One thing Chloe realized after a few cycles? Her moods had patterns.

Want to do the same? Try **a Feelings Tracker**! It can be as simple as:

= good mood
= meh mood
= irritated
= sad
= tired

Draw little faces on a calendar or use a period app with mood tracking. After two or three months, you'll probably see your own emotional pattern—and that's powerful knowledge.

(We have inserted a mood tracker for you to do just this, by the way. Check it out!)

PREMENSTRUAL SYNDROME

Let's talk about PMS—short for Premenstrual Syndrome. Sounds like something from a sci-fi movie, but really, it's just a name for the physical and emotional symptoms some people get before their period starts.

Chloe's PMS showed up like clockwork: bloating, crankiness, and a craving for sour candy and emotional support hoodies.

Not everyone has PMS, but if you do, here are some common signs:

- Mood swings or feeling extra emotional
- Headaches
- Breast tenderness
- Food cravings
- Trouble sleeping
- Feeling anxious or sad

If that sounds like you, know this: you're not broken. *Your hormones are just rearranging the furniture inside your body, and things feel a little messy for a few days.*

Chloe once said, "I wish someone told me that feeling all over the place doesn't make me broken—it makes me normal." So here's that message to you:

You're not too emotional.
You're not being dramatic.
You're just going through a cycle.
Your feelings matter.

Periods don't just affect your body.
They can affect your:

- Mood (more ups and downs than rollercoasters)
- Confidence (some days you feel unstoppable, others you just want to hide)
- Patience (hint: it might vanish)
- Focus (math during PMS? No, thank you.)

Here's how Chloe learned to deal:

- She warned her family. ("Heads up—stormy clouds incoming.")
- She gave herself permission to be low-energy.
- She planned her schedule around it —no major tasks or decisions on her "cloudy" days.

Knowing why you feel off helps you feel less overwhelmed.

And while you can't totally turn off the mood swings, you can create routines that make you feel safe, understood, and supported.

Here's what worked for Chloe:

- Talking kindly to herself, especially on sad or angry days
- Asking for hugs, quiet time, or space when needed
- Keeping a journal of "hard days" that she could look back on and say, "Hey, I survived that!"

Emotions are part of the ride—but they don't have to drive the car. You're still in control.

So take a deep breath, grab your favorite cozy hoodie, and remember: even your messiest moods are valid.

You're doing amazing. *Pinky promise.*

WORD SEARCH

Find the words listed below and circle them.

B	G	A	R	Y	T	E	N	S	I	O	N
L	C	R	A	M	P	S	B	S	E	H	V
O	E	W	S	F	Y	Y	A	A	E	B	R
A	N	E	B	T	J	S	C	T	H	T	Q
T	E	R	J	L	A	E	K	Q	N	I	R
I	R	H	G	T	J	A	P	M	D	R	K
N	G	A	H	E	A	D	A	C	H	E	R
G	Y	Y	E	R	E	L	I	E	F	D	Z
M	O	O	D	S	W	I	N	G	S	H	D

- CRAMPS
- BLOATING
- HEADACHE
- MOOD SWINGS
- ENERGY
- TIRED
- BACKPAIN
- TENSION
- RELIEF

My Feel-Better Plan

Draw, paste a picture or write one thing in each photo that helps during cramps, mood swings, or low-energy days.

Chapter 6
Food, Water, and Sleep Tips

LET'S TALK FOOD

Chloe had her period and a math test on the same day. Her cramps were acting up, her head felt foggy, and she hadn't slept well. At lunch, she skipped her veggies and grabbed fries and soda. Ten minutes later? Regret. Full-blown, bloated, cranky regret.

That's when she realized: **what you eat, drink, and how you rest can change your whole period experience.**

Your body is already working hard during your cycle—shedding the uterine lining, managing hormone shifts, and adjusting to all those emotions. *Fueling it the right way makes a big difference.*

Here's why it matters:

- Food gives your body energy to heal, balance hormones, and reduce cramps
- Water helps ease bloating and headaches (seriously, drink it!)
- Sleep lets your body rest and rebuild without it, everything feels worse

You don't need a perfect plan. You just need to notice how your body feels and give it the kindness it's asking for.

And no, you don't have to give up chocolate. We'd never ask that.

Now, let's talk food.

No, you don't need to go full "green smoothie yoga influencer" during your period. *But what you put in your body can make a real difference.*

Chloe used to grab chips, soda, and candy when cravings hit. But then she'd feel even more bloated and cranky afterward. So she started paying attention to how certain foods made her feel.

Chloe didn't go full health guru. *She just gave her body better fuel.*

Foods that Support You:

- Leafy greens (like spinach or kale): Replace lost iron and fight fatigue
- Bananas: Help with bloating and boost your mood
- Oats & whole grains: Keep your energy stable
- Nuts and seeds: Full of magnesium = less cramping
- Dark chocolate: Yes, it's real—great for your mood in moderation!

Foods to Watch Out For (a little goes a long way):

- Salty snacks: Can cause more bloating
- Sugary treats: Quick energy now, crash later
- Caffeine: Tightens blood vessels, which may make cramps worse
- Greasy fast food: Tastes amazing, feels not-so-great afterward

Chloe made simple swaps—like tea instead of soda, or trail mix instead of chips.

And *guess what*? Her cramps? Lighter. Her mood? Way more stable.

LET'S HYDRATE

Chloe used to forget to drink water—especially during her period. Then she'd get headaches, feel sluggish, and wonder why everything hurt more.

Turns out, your body needs extra hydration during your cycle.

When you're bleeding, you're losing fluids. *If you don't drink enough water, your body holds onto whatever it can.* This leads to that puffy, bloated, "ugh-my-jeans-don't-fit" feeling.

Staying hydrated helps:

- Reduce bloating
- Ease cramps
- Prevent headaches
- Boost your energy
- Help digestion (goodbye, constipation)

Simple ways to drink more water:

- Keep a cute water bottle with you (stickers = bonus motivation)
- Add fruit slices—lemon, cucumber, or berries make it fancy
- Sip herbal tea (chamomile or mint are great during your period)
- Set tiny water goals during the day: a few sips after each class, or every time you check your phone

Chloe started calling water her "liquid superpower." Not because it made her invincible, but because it helped her feel like herself again.

You don't need to chug gallons. Just sip regularly. Your body will thank you.

NAP TIME

Sleep: the most underrated period cure of all time.

Chloe used to stay up late scrolling through videos, even during her period. The next day? She was cranky, tired, and her cramps felt worse. That's when she realized—sleep isn't optional when your body's doing hard work.

During your period, your body is:

- Contracting your uterus
- Balancing hormones
- Replacing lost blood
- Managing mood swings
- And repairing itself all over

I mean, *no wonder* you feel extra tired!

Sleep tips Chloe swears by:

- Go to bed earlier on heavy flow days—your body needs the rest
- Use a heating pad while you sleep (set a timer or use one that stays warm but not hot)
- Wear comfy clothes—high-waisted sleep shorts or period undies = game changer
- Cut screen time 30 minutes before bed—your brain needs time to slow down
- Try calming rituals like journaling, stretching, or sipping warm tea before bed

Even one solid night of sleep made Chloe feel like a new person.

So when your body says "rest," don't fight it. Say yes. Snuggle in. *Give your body the reboot it needs.*

By now, Chloe had learned something big: your period doesn't just affect one part of your life—it affects your whole self.

And the secret to handling it like a pro?

Treat your body like your best friend.

That means:

- Feeding it with care and keeping it hydrated
- Letting it rest when it needs to
- Moving it gently
- And listening when it whispers "I need a break"

Chloe used to power through her period like a robot, thinking she had to "suck it up." But once she started taking care of her whole body—eating real food, drinking water, sleeping better—everything changed.

Her cramps weren't gone, but they didn't control her. Her moods still shifted, but she didn't spiral. And best of all, she felt proud, like she was finally working with her body, not against it.

So the next time your period shows up and your brain says, "I feel gross," try this instead: *"I'm doing something powerful. My body deserves support, not shame."*

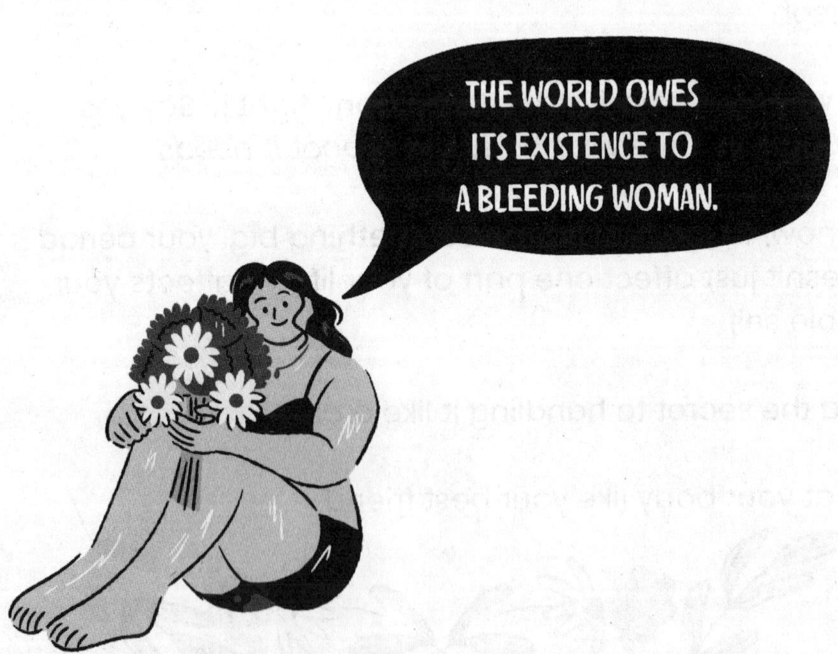

WORD SEARCH

Find the words listed below and circle them.

V	C	A	R	B	S	H	J	P	L	C	H
E	H	J	E	C	H	S	R	Y	U	Y	F
G	S	L	E	E	P	O	L	J	D	K	R
E	D	G	M	Y	T	A	W	R	V	B	U
T	R	N	E	E	F	C	A	R	B	S	I
A	R	P	I	W	A	T	E	R	S	W	T
B	B	N	G	V	I	T	A	M	I	N	S
L	Y	Q	L	O	F	R	U	I	T	S	P
E	M	I	N	E	R	A	L	S	J	T	L

- HYDRATION
- FRUITS
- VEGETABLE
- PROTEIN
- CARBS
- WATER
- SLEEP
- VITAMINS
- MINERALS

7-DAY WATER CHALLENGE

Track your water intake by filling in a droplet for each glass you drink and see how you feel after a week of staying hydrated!

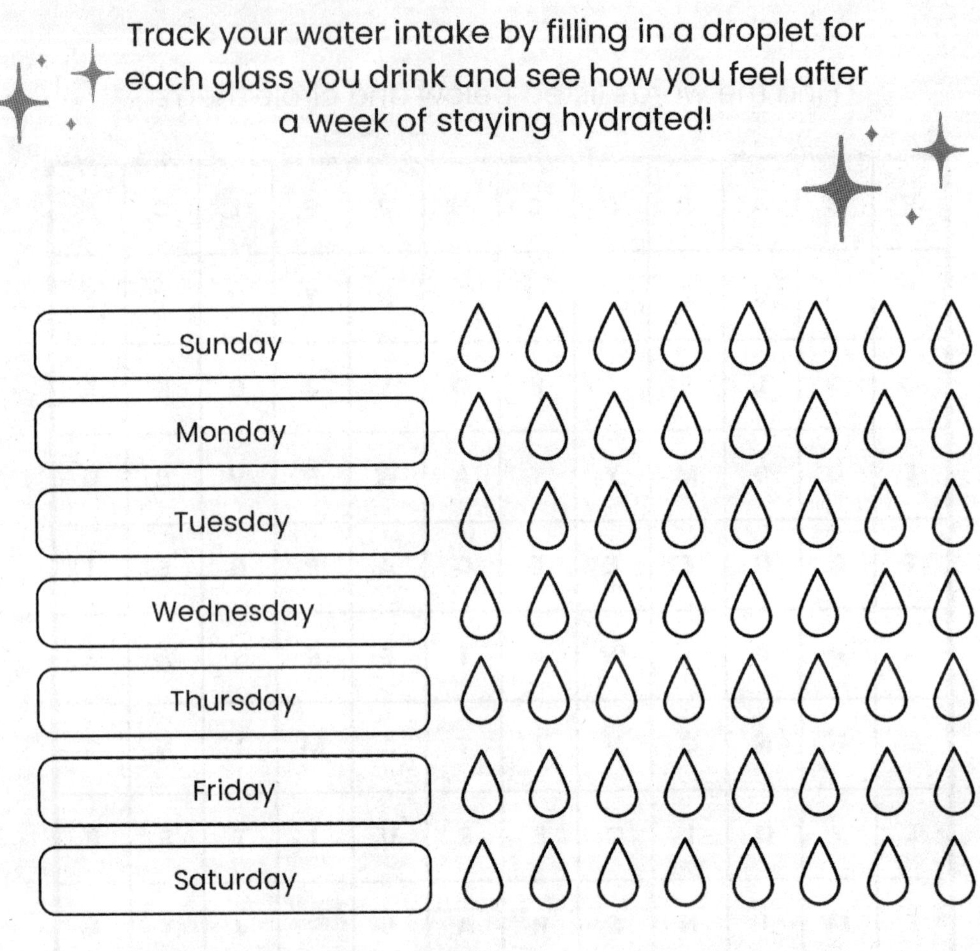

Chapter 7

Surviving School on Your Period

PERIODS AT SCHOOL

Chloe was halfway through math class when she felt it. That strange, squishy, uh-oh feeling.

Her brain immediately started yelling.

No no no no no.
Not during math.
Not while I'm wearing light-colored pants.

She shifted in her chair, trying to act normal while her heart thumped loudly in her chest. Was it her period? Was she imagining it? Should she check?

Chloe stared at the clock. Five minutes felt like five years.

If you've ever had a moment like that at school, take a slow breath.

Getting your period at school can feel extra scary. Classrooms are quiet. Chairs are light-colored. Bathroom passes feel dramatic. And you're there for hours whether you like it or not.

But remember: millions of girls have their periods at school every single day. Most of them manage just fine. After a few cycles, Chloe realized something important — school doesn't stop because of your period, but your period doesn't have to ruin school either.

It may feel big the first time. It won't always feel that way.

"CAN I GO TO THE BATHROOM?"

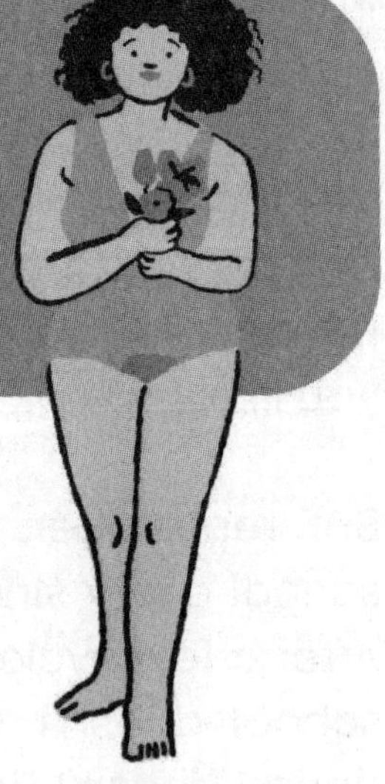

One of Chloe's biggest worries was asking to leave class.

What if she had already gone once?
What if the teacher asked why?
What if everyone stared?

Here's something important: **you do not have to explain your body to anyone.**

You can simply say, "Can I please use the restroom?"
Or, "I'm not feeling well."
Or, "I need to see the nurse."

That is enough.

You don't need to say the word "period." You don't need to give details. Your body is private, and you are allowed to take care of it.

If a teacher says, "Can it wait?" and it truly can't, it's okay to say calmly, "I really need to go. It's important." You can say it quietly and respectfully, but you can still say it firmly.

Most teachers understand more than you think. Many of them have had periods themselves, or have daughters, sisters, or friends who do. Even if they don't say it out loud, they usually know what's going on.

And if you ever feel unsure, embarrassed, or uncomfortable, the school nurse is always a safe option. You can ask to go there instead.

After one close call, Chloe decided she would always listen to her body first. Raising her hand felt scary at first, but feeling prepared felt even better.

THE SCHOOL BATHROOM MOMENT

School bathrooms can feel louder than usual when you're nervous. Wrappers seem extra crinkly. The stall door feels dramatic. Every tiny sound feels amplified.
Here's what helps: slow down.

Lock the stall. Take a breath. Check what's happening. Use your pad or liner. Wrap it neatly and throw it away in the bin. Wash your hands.

That's it.

No one is paying as much attention as you think. Most girls in that bathroom are thinking about their own day, not yours.

What If There's a Leak?

This is one of the biggest fears.

Chloe once stood up slowly from her chair and thought, Is that a shadow... or something worse?

Leaks happen. Even to grown-ups. Even to people who've had periods for years.

If it happens, **here's what you can do**:

- Tie a sweatshirt or jacket around your waist.
- Go to the bathroom or nurse.
- Change if you can.
- If you can't, remember that most stains wash out.

And here's something many girls realize later: most people don't notice. And if they do, they usually don't make a big deal about it.

It feels huge in the moment. It rarely is.

SCHOOL UNIFORMS & LIGHT-COLORED CLOTHES

White skirts. Khaki pants. Light grey uniforms.

Why do they always seem to appear during period week?

There is something about light-colored clothes that can make your brain go into "what if" mode. Even if everything is completely fine, you might catch yourself thinking, *What if there's a stain? What if I stand up and something shows? What if I didn't notice?*

Chloe once sat through an entire class barely moving because she was wearing beige pants. She was so focused on staying perfectly still that she missed half the lesson. When she finally checked later, there was nothing there at all.

If you wear a uniform or light clothing, **a few small habits can help you feel more secure:**

- Wear darker underwear under light clothing for extra peace of mind.
- Change your pad more often on heavier days, especially at recess or lunchtime.
- Use pads with wings so they stay in place while you sit and stand.
- Make sure your pad is centered properly before leaving the bathroom.
- Wear snug shorts or bike shorts under skirts if your school allows it — this can add an extra layer of protection.

And here's something important: **clothes are meant to fit your life**. If your uniform feels uncomfortable or too tight while your body is changing, it's okay to tell a parent or trusted adult. Bodies grow. Sizes change. That's normal.

These habits don't mean you expect something bad to happen. They simply mean you're prepared.

Light-colored clothes don't get to decide how your day goes. Preparation builds confidence. And confidence lets you focus on school instead of constantly wondering, *What if*?

Chloe eventually realized that confidence doesn't come from wearing dark clothes. It comes from knowing she could handle whatever happened.

BORROWING A TAMPON

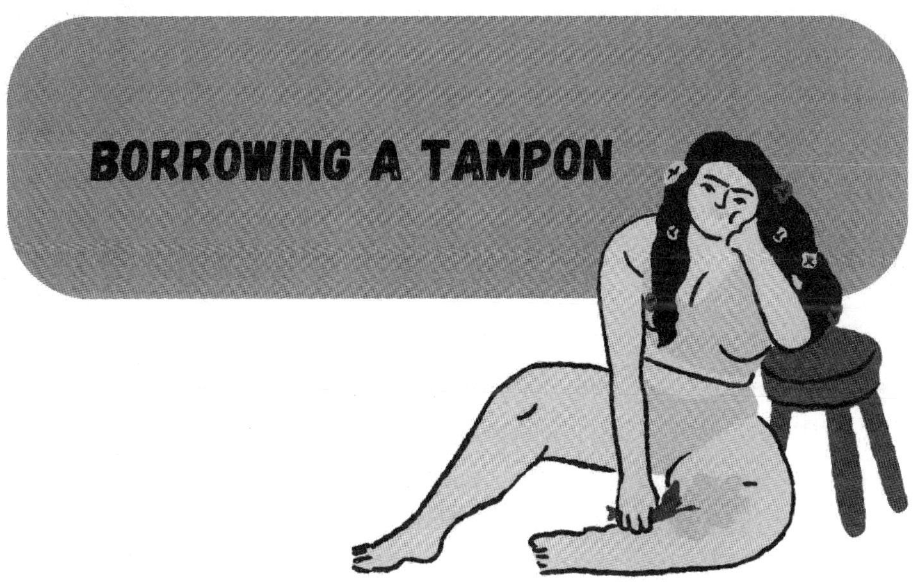

One afternoon in the school bathroom, Chloe heard a small voice from the next stall.

"Um... does anyone have a tampon?"

There was a pause. The kind of pause where everyone pretends they didn't hear. Chloe felt her heart beat a little faster. She knew that voice. It sounded nervous. Embarrassed. Maybe even close to tears.

For a second, Chloe froze. Then she reached into her backpack pouch and quietly said, "I do."

She slid one under the stall door.

The relief on the other girl's face when she came out was almost instant. She smiled and whispered, "Thank you."

Borrowing or lending a pad is one of the most normal things in the world. It might feel dramatic in your head, but in real life, it's usually quick and simple. Most girls understand exactly how it feels to be unprepared.

If you ever need to ask, you can keep it quiet and simple.

You might say,

- "Does anyone have a tampon I can borrow?"
- Or even just, "Can someone help me?"

You don't have to explain anything else.

And if you don't have one to lend someday? That's okay too. You can help by walking with a friend to the nurse or helping her feel less alone.

FIELD TRIPS & LONG SCHOOL DAYS

Field trips are supposed to be exciting.

The bus ride. The snacks. The museum gift shop. The zoo. The science center. The big yellow permission slip.

But if your period shows up on the same day? Suddenly the excitement can turn into worry.

Chloe once had a field trip to a history museum an hour away from school. The night before, she realized her period might start. Her brain immediately went into panic mode.

What if there's no bathroom on the bus?
What if I need to change during the tour?

All it takes is a little planning and you can handle a field trip on your period like a pro!

When you know you'll be away from school longer than usual, preparation is your best friend.

A few simple things that might help:

- **Pack extra supplies** (at least 2–3 pads, even if you think you won't need them).
- **Bring a small pouch** to keep everything private and easy to grab.
- **Use the bathroom before getting on the bus**, even if you don't feel like you have to.
- **Change your pad before leaving school** for the trip.
- **Wear comfortable, secure underwear and darker bottoms**.

Long school days, like testing days or assemblies, can feel similar. You might not have as many chances to leave the room. Bathrooms might be busier. Schedules might change.

That's why checking in with your body during breaks is important. If there's a lunch break or transition time, use it.

If you ever feel nervous about asking to use the restroom during a trip, remember: teachers know kids have real needs. You don't have to announce anything. A simple, "Can I please use the restroom?" is enough.

Just know that even if something doesn't go perfectly, it won't ruin the whole day. You can fix small problems. You can adjust. You can move on.

Chloe ended up having a great time at the museum. She checked in with herself, used the restroom when she needed to, and focused on the fun parts.

WORD SEARCH

Find the words listed below and circle them.

B	K	P	R	E	P	A	R	E	A	A	Z
A	D	R	L	L	A	H	F	F	C	F	S
T	R	I	W	A	H	G	R	H	H	N	U
H	Q	V	N	Z	N	M	I	R	Y	J	P
R	N	A	K	S	F	S	E	P	F	Y	P
O	K	C	A	H	Y	K	N	I	S	N	L
O	R	Y	I	M	C	W	D	F	N	F	I
M	S	C	H	O	O	L	S	N	N	N	E
L	P	C	L	A	S	S	R	O	O	M	S

- LOCKER
- SCHOOL
- BATHROOM
- CLASSROOM
- PRIVACY
- PLAN
- FRIENDS
- PREPARE
- SUPPLIES

MY CALM & CONFIDENT SCHOOL SCRIPT

Practice what to say so you prepared at school.

1. May I please go to the ________________ ?

2. I'm not feeling well and need a quick break to ________________________.

3. I'm having cramps, so I need to __________ ________________________.

4. I'll be back in a few minutes after I _______ ________________________.

5. I brought ________________________ in case I needed it.

6. Can you come with me to the __________ ________________________?

7. I just started my period and feel _________ ________________________.

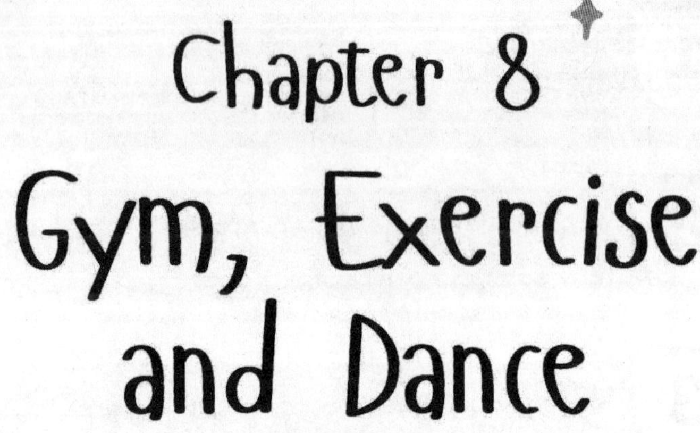

Chapter 8
Gym, Exercise and Dance

YES, YOU CAN STILL MOVE

Chloe loved Wednesdays.

Wednesdays were dance days.

But this Wednesday felt different.

She was tying her sneakers in the locker room when she felt that familiar cramp in her belly.

Seriously? she thought. *Today*?

They were learning a new routine. There would be jumps. And turns. And everyone would be watching in the mirror. For a second, Chloe thought about telling her mom she felt sick. Or asking her teacher if she could sit out.

But then she remembered something important: she still liked moving. She still liked dancing. Her period didn't change that.

Some people think that when you have your period, you're supposed to lie down and not move at all.

That's not true.

You are allowed to run.
You are allowed to stretch.
You are allowed to dance, jump, and play.

Moving your body during your period is safe. In fact, gentle movement can actually help your body feel better.

The key word is gentle. You don't have to go faster or harder than usual. You just have to listen to your body.

WHY EXERCISE CAN HELP

When you have your period, it can feel like the best idea is to curl up on the couch and not move at all. And sometimes, resting is the right choice.

That being said, gentle exercise can actually help your body feel better during your period.

When you move, your body releases special "**feel-good**" chemicals in your brain. These chemicals can help improve your mood and make cramps feel less intense.

That doesn't mean you have to run a mile or do a hard workout. Even stretching, walking, or light dancing in your room counts.

Chloe noticed this during dance class. Before practice, her stomach felt tight and uncomfortable. But once she started warming up, slowly her body felt looser. The cramps didn't completely disappear, but they didn't feel as overwhelming.

Movement works because it helps your body in several ways:

- **It increases blood flow**, which can help relax the muscles in your lower belly where cramps happen.
- **It releases endorphins**, which are natural chemicals that boost your mood and help reduce pain.
- **It reduces bloating**, because gentle movement helps your digestion.
- **It lowers stress**, and less stress can mean fewer uncomfortable symptoms.
- **It helps you sleep better**, which makes everything feel easier the next day.

Even five or ten minutes of light stretching, a short walk, or a calm bike ride can make a difference. Listen to your body. Move in a way that feels good — not forced.

You might notice that some days you feel totally fine and full of energy. Other days, you might feel slower or more tired. That's normal. Your period can change how your body feels from day to day.

Instead of asking, "Can I keep up?" try asking, "What does my body need right now?"

Maybe it needs a few deep breaths before class starts.
Maybe it needs a slower warm-up.
Maybe it just needs you to believe it can handle this.

Your body isn't working against you. It's working with you — even on period days.

GYM CLASS AT SCHOOL

Gym class on your period can feel like a big deal.

There's running. There's stretching. Sometimes there are light-colored gym shorts. And sometimes it feels like everyone is watching — even though they probably aren't.

Chloe used to worry most about two things: leaks and cramps. She didn't want to be the girl who had to stop in the middle of a game. She didn't want to feel uncomfortable while everyone else seemed fine.

What helped her the most wasn't pretending everything was okay. It was preparing ahead of time.

Before gym class, a little planning can make a big difference:

- **Wear darker underwear under your gym clothes**, even if the shorts are light.
- **Double-check that your pad is centered and secure** before leaving the locker room.
- **Learn where the closest restroom is**, so you don't waste time if you need it.

These small steps can help you feel calmer before you even step onto the gym floor.

If your cramps are bothering you, warming up slowly can help. Try stretching your legs gently. Roll your shoulders. Take a few deep breaths before the activity starts. Sometimes your body just needs a few extra minutes to adjust.

If you start feeling uncomfortable during class, you have options. You don't have to suffer in silence. You can:

- **Walk instead of run** for a lap or two.
- **Raise your hand and ask for a quick restroom break**.
- **Tell your teacher privately that you're not feeling well**.
- **Ask to sit out for a few minutes if you feel dizzy or crampy**.
- **Get a drink of water**, which can sometimes ease discomfort.

If you're worried about light-colored shorts, check yourself in the locker room mirror before class. On heavier days, you might feel more comfortable wearing darker leggings if your school allows them. If not, preparation and secure placement are your best tools

It's also important to know when to truly rest. Mild cramps are common, but if you feel sharp pain, dizziness, or like you might faint, tell a teacher right away and visit the nurse.

Gym class is about learning skills and staying active, not proving anything. Some days you'll feel strong and fast. Other days you'll move a little slower. Both are completely normal.

DANCE CLASS & TIGHT CLOTHES

Dance class can feel different from gym class.

Leotards. Tights. Fitted leggings. Sometimes even light-colored costumes.

There isn't much room to "hide," and that can make you extra aware of your body, especially during your period.

Chloe loved dance, but the first time she had her period during class, she felt nervous the entire warm-up.

Every kick felt dramatic. Every turn made her wonder, Is everything staying in place? She kept adjusting her tights and barely focused on the choreography.

What she learned over time is that tight dance clothes don't automatically mean something will go wrong. They just mean you need to be a little more thoughtful before class starts.

Because dance clothes are more fitted, it's important to start class feeling secure. Choosing a thin pad with wings can make movement more comfortable and help prevent shifting during jumps or turns.

It's also helpful to use the restroom even if you don't urgently need to, just to check that everything feels centered and secure. A quick mirror check in the dressing room can calm your nerves before stepping onto the floor.

Dance involves stretching, floor work, leaps, and sometimes fast turns. If something feels slightly uncomfortable during warm-up, it's okay to fix it early rather than worrying about it for the rest of class.

Dance involves stretching, floor work, leaps, and sometimes fast turns. If something feels slightly uncomfortable during warm-up, it's okay to fix it early rather than worrying about it for the rest of class.

If you start feeling unsure during class, here are simple things you can do:

- **Use a water break** to quickly visit the restroom if needed.
- **Make jumps or movements smaller** for a few minutes if cramps feel strong.
- **Stand toward the side or back** during across-the-floor work if that eases anxiety.
- **Take slow, steady breaths** during deep stretches to relax belly muscles.
- **Quietly ask your instructor for a short break** if you truly need one.

Cramps can feel more noticeable during backbends or core exercises. Gentle movement often helps, but sharp pain is a signal to pause. Listening to your body is part of being a strong dancer.

Keep in mind that everyone else is thinking about their own steps. They're counting, balancing, trying not to fall out of a turn. They are not studying you.

When Chloe finally focused on the music instead of her worries, she realized her body could still leap, spin, and stretch beautifully.

Your period doesn't take away your rhythm, your strength, or your ability to shine. Even in tights under bright studio lights.

WHAT ABOUT SPORTS?

Sports on your period can feel dramatic in your head: What if I'm slower? What if I mess up?

Meanwhile, everyone else is mostly thinking about the score, the coach, or whether they remembered their water bottle.

Chloe plays basketball, and the first time she had her period during a game, she was sure it would ruin everything. She imagined herself running in slow motion while the other team zoomed past her.

That didn't happen.

What did happen was that she felt slightly more tired than usual. And that's actually very normal. Hormones shift during your cycle, which can affect energy levels.

Some days you'll feel powerful and fast. Other days you might feel steady but not super speedy. That doesn't mean something is wrong, it just means your body isn't the same every single day of the month.

Instead of trying to play exactly the same way every time, it helps to play smart.

On lower-energy days, you can:

- **Focus on positioning instead of speed,** being in the right place matters more than being the fastest.
- **Talk more to your teammates** so you're working together instead of doing everything yourself.
- **Accept substitutions when offered** instead of pushing past exhaustion.
- **Slow the game down in your mind** — steady passes and clear decisions beat rushed ones.
- **Use time-outs to breathe deeply and reset**, not to criticize yourself.

That's not weakness. That's strategy.

Cramps are another common worry. Quick turns, sprinting, or jumping can sometimes make your belly feel tight at first.

What helps most is giving your body a proper warm-up. A few extra minutes of jogging, stretching your hips and thighs, and gently twisting your torso can loosen muscles before the game really starts.

Away games and tournaments can feel more stressful because you're out of your routine. A simple trick? When you arrive, casually notice where the bathrooms are. You don't have to tell anyone why. Just knowing where they are removes one big "what if" from your brain.

Sports are already unpredictable. People trip. People miss shots. People feel tired. That's part of being human, not part of having a period

Over time, you'll start noticing your own patterns. Maybe you feel strongest a few days into your cycle. Maybe you need a slower first quarter and a stronger finish. That awareness makes you a smarter athlete.

KNOWING WHEN TO REST

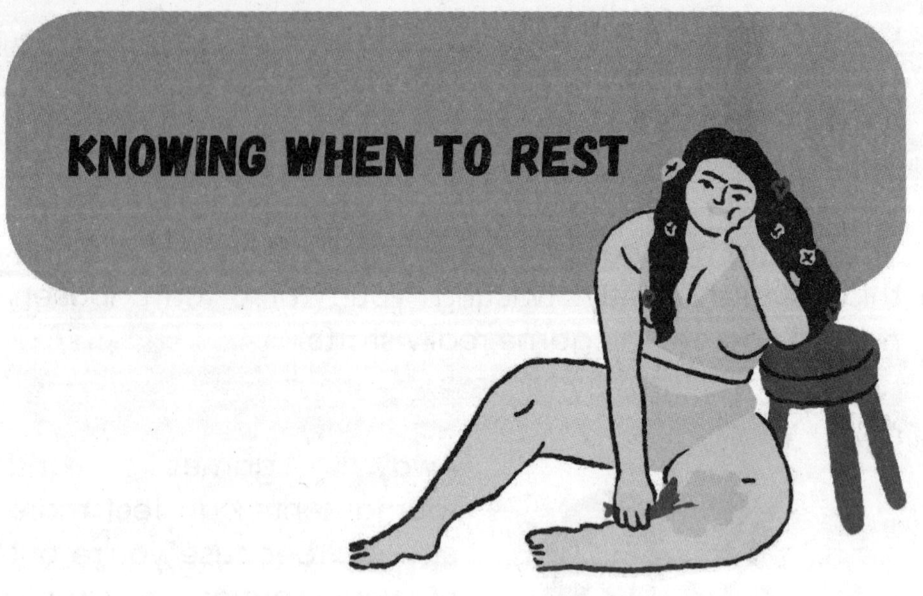

There's a big difference between quitting and resting.

Quitting is giving up because something feels hard.

Resting is choosing to pause because your body needs care.

During your period, your body is working behind the scenes. Your uterus is shedding its lining, your hormones are shifting, and your energy might dip.

That's real physical work, even if no one can see it.

Chloe used to think she had to push through everything. If she felt tired during practice, she ignored it. If her cramps felt sharp, she told herself to "just deal with it."

But she learned something important: pushing through every signal doesn't make you stronger. Sometimes it just makes you more exhausted.

The first step is learning the difference between normal discomfort and a sign to pause.

Mild cramps, a slightly heavy feeling, or low energy? Those are common and manageable.

Sharp pain, dizziness, nausea, or feeling like you might faint? That's your body clearly asking for a break.

When you decide to rest, keep this small things in mind:

- **Sit upright** instead of curling tightly forward, which can sometimes increase belly pressure.
- **Use steady, slow breathing** (in for four counts, out for four) to relax abdominal muscles.
- **Place a warm heating pad** on your lower belly at home to ease muscle tension.
- **Stretch gently** instead of lying completely still if cramps feel tight rather than sharp.
- **Drink small sips of water** regularly, especially if you feel lightheaded.

Rest doesn't always mean sleeping for hours. Sometimes it means adjusting your activity level for the day.

On heavy or extra-crampy days, you might:

- **Switch intense workouts for light movement**, like walking or easy stretching.
- **Go to bed 30–60 minutes earlier** than usual.
- **Eat regular meals** even if you don't feel super hungry, low energy can feel worse on an empty stomach.
- **Limit very sugary snacks**, which can make energy crash later.
- **Check in with a trusted adult** if pain feels stronger than usual.

It's also helpful to notice patterns. If you track how you feel for a few months, you might see that certain days of your cycle are more tiring than others. That helps you plan ahead instead of feeling surprised.

Rest is not a weakness in sports or in life. Professional athletes build rest days into their schedules on purpose. Muscles repair during rest. Energy rebuilds during rest. Your body balances itself during rest.

WORD SEARCH

Find the words listed below and circle them.

F	A	E	N	D	O	R	P	H	I	N	S
M	F	X	F	I	T	N	E	S	S	I	T
D	G	E	L	D	B	A	F	M	T	B	R
J	C	R	H	T	A	M	P	L	F	S	E
L	A	C	D	U	L	F	U	W	Y	T	T
Y	R	I	A	N	A	B	M	S	K	A	C
I	D	S	N	S	N	D	K	B	C	W	H
P	I	E	C	B	C	N	L	G	L	L	H
M	O	V	E	M	E	N	T	B	E	G	E

- STRETCH
- ENDORPHINS
- MOVEMENT
- EXERCISE
- FITNESS
- CARDIO
- DANCE
- MUSCLE
- BALANCE

BINGO

Mark each square that feels true for you

WORRIED ABOUT LEAKING DURING GYM CLASS	FELT NERVOUS CHANGING IN THE LOCKER ROOM	STRETCHED TO HELP EASE CRAMPS
NOTICED THAT MOVEMENT HELPED BOOST MOOD	MY BODY IS STRONG	DANCED ANYWAY, EVEN WHILE FEELING BLOATED
ADJUSTED A WORKOUT BASED ON ENERGY LEVELS	TOOK A BREAK WHEN THE BODY NEEDED REST	ASKED TO USE THE BATHROOM DURING CLASS

Chapter 9
Body Image and Growing Confidence

GROWING INTO YOU

Chloe didn't mean to stare at herself that long.

She was brushing her hair before school when she caught her reflection and paused.

Her face looked the same. But her body?

Her clothes fit differently. Her shoulders looked a little wider. Her chest wasn't flat anymore. Even the way she stood felt unfamiliar.

Was I always shaped like this?

If you've ever had this moment, you're not weird.

You're growing.

And growth comes with changes that are real, biological, and completely normal.

PUBERTY WEIGHT GAIN & YOUR BODY'S BLUEPRINT

One afternoon, Chloe was trying on jeans that had fit perfectly a few months ago.

Now they didn't.

She tugged at the waistband. She turned sideways. She sucked in her stomach (even though she didn't really know why she was doing that). The jeans weren't "too small," they just fit differently.

Her hips felt wider. Her thighs touched when she walked. Her stomach felt softer than it used to.

Her first thought was: *Did I do something wrong?*

The answer is simple.

No.

During puberty, girls' bodies naturally gain weight — especially body fat. This isn't random. It isn't a mistake. It's not caused by eating one extra snack or skipping one practice.

It's biology.

Before puberty, girls and boys have fairly similar body shapes. But during puberty, girls' bodies begin storing more fat in certain areas, including:

- Hips
- Thighs
- Chest
- Buttocks
- Lower stomach

This fat isn't "bad." It isn't "extra." It's necessary.

Your body needs a certain amount of fat to:

- Produce and regulate hormones
- Support the start of your menstrual cycle
- Protect internal organs
- Store energy for rapid growth

Without enough body fat, puberty can actually slow down or pause. That's how important it is.

Now let's talk about something just as important: **genetics**.

Chloe once noticed that her best friend had narrow hips and long, lean legs. Another friend had broader shoulders. Another developed earlier. Another later.

Same age. Completely different bodies.

Why?

Because every body comes with its own blueprint.

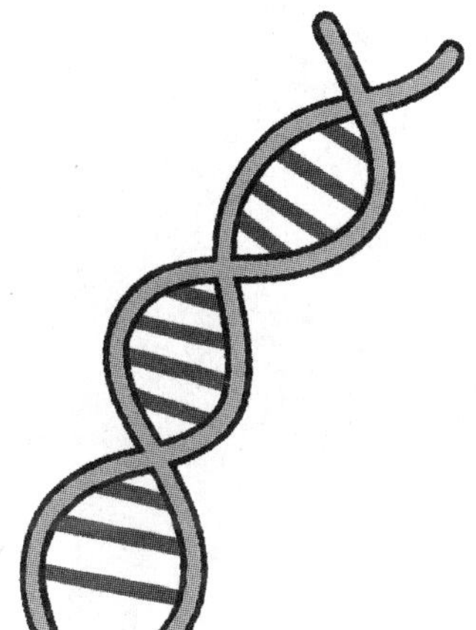

Your genetics, which are the traits passed down from your family, influence:

- Your height
- Your body shape
- Where you store fat
- How quickly you develop
- Your bone structure
- Your muscle build

If many women in your family have curvier hips, you might too. If they're tall, you might be tall. If they develop earlier, you might as well.

You did not choose this blueprint.

And you cannot trade it in.

Comparing your body to someone with a completely different genetic background is like comparing two different breeds of dogs and asking why they don't look identical. They aren't supposed to.

Some bodies are naturally straight-shaped.
Some are curvier.
Some are muscular.
Some are softer.

None of those shapes are "better." They're different designs.

Here's another fact that surprises many girls: during puberty, your body may gain weight before you grow taller. It's common for the body to store energy first, then use it during a growth spurt.

That means you might feel "bigger" for a little while, and then suddenly grow several inches taller.

Bodies don't grow in neat, predictable order.

They grow in phases.

Chloe eventually realized something important: the parts of her body she worried about most were the same parts that made her strong on the basketball court. Her sturdy legs helped her pivot. Her hips helped her balance. Her body wasn't working against her, it was building her.

Puberty is not about shrinking yourself into a smaller version of who you were.

It's about expanding into who you're becoming.

Your body's blueprint isn't random. It's inherited and purposeful.

Understanding that doesn't mean you'll love every change instantly. But it does mean you can stop blaming yourself for growth that was always meant to happen.

THE COMPARISON TRAP

Chloe wasn't even trying to compare herself.

She was just standing in line at school when she noticed something.

Emma was taller.
Maya had longer hair.
Sophie seemed to have "perfect" skin.
Lila's sneakers were the cool kind everyone wanted.

And suddenly, Chloe wasn't just standing in line anymore.

She was measuring.

Am I taller or shorter?
Why don't my legs look like that?
Should my hair look like hers?

If this has ever happened to you, welcome to something very normal: comparison.

Around ages 8 to 12, your brain becomes extra good at noticing differences. It's part of growing up. You start understanding social groups more. You notice trends. You become aware of who stands out and why.

Your brain thinks it's being helpful. It's gathering information.

But here's the problem: comparison rarely makes you feel better.

It's like your brain opens a scoreboard you never asked for.

Height: *check.*
Clothes: *check.*
Hair: *check.*
Popularity: *check.*

Except, there's no actual prize. No winner. No trophy for "Most Like Someone Else."

Comparison also has a funny habit: it only looks one direction.

You might compare yourself to someone you think is "ahead" in some way be it taller, faster, more confident. But you rarely compare in the other direction.

You don't usually think, "Wow, I'm really strong in math compared to that person," or "I'm a kinder friend than that girl."

The girl you think has "perfect skin" might be worrying about her braces. The tall girl might wish she were shorter. The athletic girl might feel nervous every time she competes.

Everyone has something.

If you catch yourself comparing, pause and ask, "*Is this helpful?*" and if it's not, shift your focus to something your body can do or something you're proud of.

SOCIAL MEDIA AND THE PERFECT ILLUSION

Chloe was supposed to be finishing her science worksheet.

Instead, she was "just checking one video." One turned into five. Five turned into fifteen.

A girl her age was showing her morning routine with glowing skin and perfectly brushed hair. Another posted a dance video that looked completely effortless. Someone else shared a photo in a spotless bedroom with fairy lights and matching bedding.

Chloe glanced at her own reflection in the dark screen when the video paused.

Her ponytail was lumpy. She had a small pimple near her nose. Her room definitely did not look like a magazine.

She hadn't felt bad before. But now she did.

Nothing mean had happened. No one had said anything unkind. But comparison had quietly slipped in.

Most of what you see online is a highlight reel. People usually post their best angles, best lighting, best moments. You're seeing the polished pieces — not the whole story.

And sometimes, you're not even seeing reality.

Filters can smooth skin. Lighting can blur texture. Certain camera angles can make someone look taller or slimmer. Some apps can even subtly reshape facial features or body proportions without it being obvious.

So when you compare yourself to what you're seeing, you might actually be comparing yourself to something edited.

There's another layer too. Social media apps are designed to notice what holds your attention. If you pause on beauty videos or appearance-related posts, the app sends you more of them. Soon your feed can start to look like everyone in the world has perfect skin and flawless hair.

But that's not real life.

If you ever notice that after scrolling you feel smaller, more critical, or suddenly unhappy with your body, that's useful information. It means something you're consuming isn't helping you.

You can actually take control of that.

- **Unfollow accounts** that make you feel small.
- **Follow creators who teach skills** or hobbies.
- **Take breaks** when scrolling starts to feel heavy.
- **Remember that filters exist** even when you can't see them.

Chloe eventually noticed something interesting.

She never felt worse about herself while drawing, running, laughing with friends, or learning something new.

It only happened when she spent too long staring at edited squares on a screen.

Social media can be funny, creative, and inspiring. It's not the enemy. But it isn't a mirror either.

Your real life includes messy ponytails, regular bedrooms, awkward angles, and unfiltered skin.

And that's not something to fix.

BUILDING REAL CONFIDENCE

Chloe used to think confidence was something you either had or didn't.

Like some girls were just born with it.

They raised their hands easily. They walked into rooms like they belonged there. They didn't seem to overthink every little thing.

Chloe thought, *Maybe I'm just not the confident type.*

The thing about confidence is that, **it isn't a personality trait**. It's more like a skill.

And skills can be built.

Confidence doesn't usually come from staring in the mirror and deciding you look amazing. It grows from doing things, especially things that feel a little uncomfortable at first

Confidence grows when you:

- **Practice something** and see yourself improve
- **Try again** after messing up
- **Keep promises** you make to yourself
- **Spend time with people** who are kind and supportive
- **Do hard things** and realize you survived them

Notice something? None of those have anything to do with having perfect hair or the "right" body shape.

Confidence grows from action.

For example, Chloe didn't suddenly feel confident about basketball by wishing for it. She felt more confident after practicing free throws over and over, even the ones she missed. Every small improvement told her brain, *Hey, I can get better at things*.

However, sometimes confidence dips lower than usual. And that's okay too.

There's a difference between having an "off day" and feeling stuck in negative thoughts.

If you notice that you:

- **Avoid things** you used to enjoy
- **Think about your appearance** almost all day
- **Feel embarrassed** or ashamed most of the time
- **Change how you eat or act** because you dislike your body
- **Feel like you're never "good enough"** no matter what

That's a sign you might need backup and getting backup is not weakness, it's smart.

Talking to a parent, caregiver, school counselor, teacher, or doctor can really help. Sometimes just saying your worries out loud makes them feel smaller. Other times, a trusted adult can give you tools to handle those thoughts better.

You don't have to figure everything out alone.

WORD SEARCH

Find the words listed below and circle them.

F	G	D	E	U	I	A	R	N	U	E	R
H	F	Q	P	R	O	U	D	W	R	T	E
U	G	N	S	E	L	F	L	O	V	E	S
N	I	D	F	S	B	E	A	U	T	Y	P
I	E	A	J	P	O	S	I	T	I	V	E
Q	H	L	T	E	D	F	S	N	M	H	C
U	K	H	A	C	Y	Y	L	O	A	E	T
E	O	H	N	T	O	I	A	M	G	L	Y
C	O	N	F	I	D	E	N	C	E	O	I

- CONFIDENCE
- BEAUTY
- RESPECT
- POSITIVE
- UNIQUE
- SELF LOVE
- PROUD
- BODY
- IMAGE

Compliment Yourself

Write a compliment about yourself that is NOT about how you look.

1. I am brave when...

2. A challenge I've overcome is...

3. What makes me unique is...

4. I am kind because...

5. I am getting better at...

Chapter 10
Your Period Kit

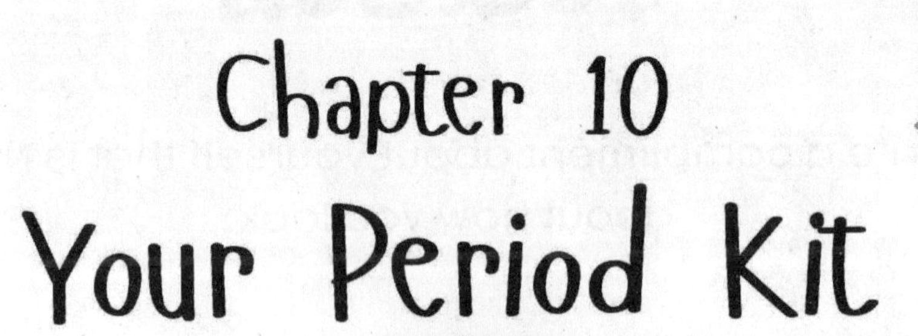

WHAT TO KEEP IN YOUR BAG

Chloe was in gym class when she felt a familiar, dreaded squish. She hadn't expected her period for another three days. Panic mode: activate.

She checked her bag. Inside? Nothing. No pad, no spare underwear, no clue what to do.

That day changed everything—because after that, Chloe built the ultimate period kit.

Every girl deserves a little backup plan for when Aunt Flo drops in unexpectedly. Whether it's your backpack, locker, sports bag, or purse, having your own period pouch = instant peace of mind.

You don't need a fancy setup. Just a small makeup bag, pencil case, or even a ziplock pouch works great.

Think of your period kit as your "I got this" bag. Because with the right stuff on hand, you do got this.

So... what actually goes in a period kit?

Chloe figured it out the hard way after one too many "oops" moments. You can get it right the first time.

Here's what Chloe always includes:

- 2–3 pads: A mix of regular and overnight sizes
- 1–2 pantyliners: For light days or spotting
- 1 spare pair of underwear: Because leaks happen
- Wipes: Unscented is best—
  great for feeling fresh
- A small plastic bag: For wrapping used underwear or products
- Hand sanitizer: Especially if the school bathroom is out of soap
- Mini chocolate bar or snack: Because moods need love too

She also keeps a folded-up sticky note inside with a kind message to herself:
**"You're okay.
You've got this.
Just breathe."**

The point of the kit isn't to be fancy. It's to help you feel prepared, calm, and confident. Like a period ninja with her tools always nearby. If you don't like the idea of carrying it everywhere, all the time, just keep track of your cycle and bring it along only when you're near your date.

Chloe's favorite thing about her period kit? It made her feel in control. Before she had one, her period felt like this giant unpredictable thing. But once she had her kit? Instant confidence boost.

She even decorated it with stickers (a glittery lightning bolt and a tiny dinosaur), because why not? If you're going to carry a mini emergency pack, it may as well match your vibe.

Want to know the coolest thing about building your own period kit? You're creating a little reminder that says:
"I care about me."

Once Chloe had her pouch packed, she zipped it closed, held it up like a trophy, and declared, "I am now officially unstoppable."

Okay, maybe not *unstoppable,* but she definitely felt more calm, more confident, and way less panicky about surprise periods.

Still deciding what to include?

Pro tip: test-drive your kit at home first. Wear a pad from your kit. Try opening a wrapper quietly (school bathrooms echo, lol). Check if your pouch fits in your backpack without taking up all the space.

Make adjustments:

- Too bulky? Switch to pantyliners or thinner pads
- No room for snacks? Try a small pack of nuts or a granola bar
- Want more privacy? Wrap your kit in a scrunchie or hoodie pocket
- Play around with what you need after you've got the hang of it. You can carry bare essentials around the time of your due date and add more items when you're actually on your period.

And if you ever forget it? Don't stress. Ask a friend, a teacher, or the nurse.

That tiny pouch in your backpack? It's more than just pads and snacks. It's a soft place to land when your period surprises you. It's proof that you're smart, prepared, and showing up for yourself—even on the tough days.

Here's Chloe's top advice:

- <u>Don't wait for a disaster</u>—pack your kit before you need it.
- <u>Keep it stocked</u>—if you use something, replace it when you get home.
- <u>Tell a trusted friend where it is</u>—period besties stick together.
- **<u>Repack it</u>** every few months. (Expired chocolate? Ew.)

Remember, it's YOUR kit. You can update it as you grow, switch from pads to tampons, or try new things. Chloe even kept a backup kit in her locker and her sleepover bag.

So whether your kit fits in a sparkly pencil case or a zipped hoodie pocket—it counts.

Basic Essentials

- [ ] 2-3 pads (regular or overnight... or both)
- [ ] 1-2 pantyliners
- [ ] 1 clean pair of underwear
- [ ] A few unscented wipes
- [ ] Travel-size hand sanitizer
- [ ] Pain reliever

Optional (Or Basic Pt.2)

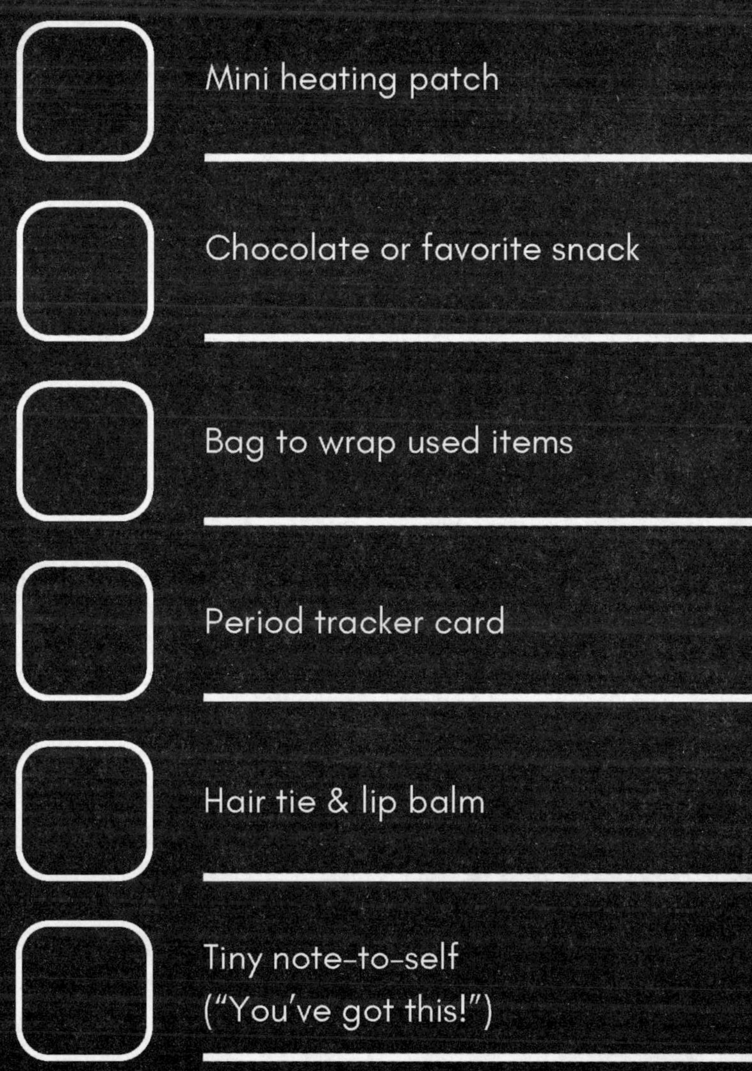

- [ ] Mini heating patch
- [ ] Chocolate or favorite snack
- [ ] Bag to wrap used items
- [ ] Period tracker card
- [ ] Hair tie & lip balm
- [ ] Tiny note-to-self ("You've got this!")

HANDLING EMERGENCIES LIKE A PRO

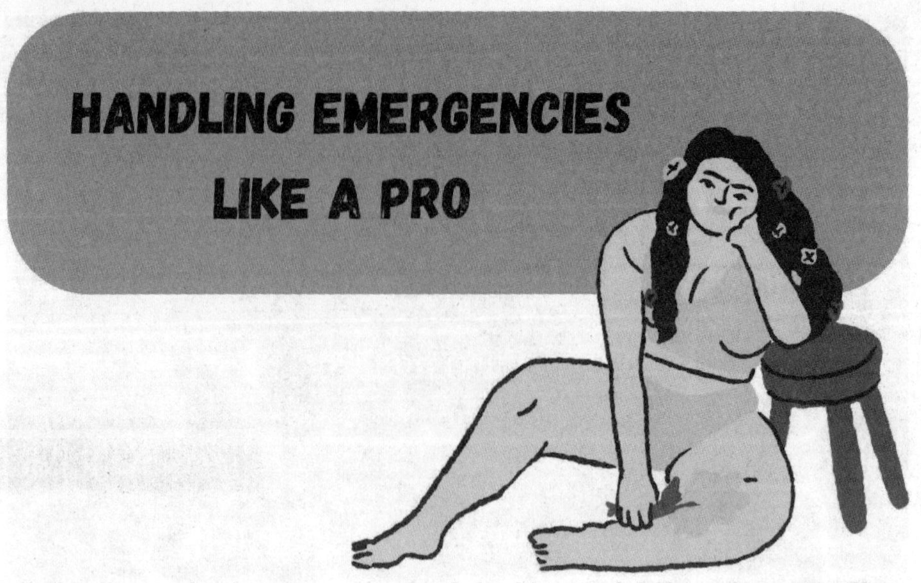

Chloe's period once started in the middle of a spelling bee.

She was wearing light jeans. No kit. No clue. Just panic.

At first, she froze. Then she whispered to her teammate, "I think I got my period." Her teammate didn't freak out. She just nodded, handed her a sweatshirt, and walked her to the bathroom like a total legend.

That was the moment Chloe realized: *you can handle period emergencies without freaking out*. You just need a few smart moves.

Let's talk about what to do when your period shows up uninvited and unprepared.

Step 1: Don't panic

Seriously—just breathe. You're not in danger. A little blood can feel like a lot, but you're okay.

Step 2: Excuse yourself

Ask to go to the bathroom. You don't have to explain why. Just go.

Step 3: Assess the situation

Check your underwear and clothes. Is it just starting? Is there a stain? You've got options either way.

Pro Tip: Most emergencies are way less dramatic than your brain makes them out to be.

Okay, you've made it to the bathroom—now what?

Chloe always says:
"Be a bathroom MacGyver."
Even if you don't have your kit, you can still figure it out.

If you don't have a pad or tampon, **you can DIY one!**

- Wrap toiler paper sheets around the gusset (that's the crotch area) of your underwear
- Fold a clean paper towel or tissue and layer it in
- Fold the tissue and toilet paper into a rectangle and wrap another layer around it to keep it in place

Not ideal? True. But it'll get you through the next class until you can grab something better.

If you leaked onto your clothes:

- Wrap a sweatshirt or jacket around your waist
- Ask a friend if they have anything extra
- Head to the nurse's office—most schools keep pads, clean underwear, and even spare pants
- Don't feel embarrassed. This happens to everyone.

Chloe once leaked on her leggings in gym class. She thought she'd die. But guess what? No one laughed. Her friends backed her up. She changed. Life moved on.

It's not the end of the world. It's just a smudge—and it'll wash out.

Chloe learned a golden rule: **someone always has what you need—if you just ask.**

Asking for a pad or tampon can feel awkward at first. But you know what? *Most people want to help. And they probably remember needing help once, too.*

Even if you forget your kit... even if you leak... even if you have a total surprise start...
You've got options.
You've got people.
You've got YOU.

Chloe keeps one last thing in her pouch: a folded note that says, **"Dear Me, I'm proud of you. You handled this like a champ."**

You can write one too.

Because emergency or not, every time you listen to your body, take care of yourself, and keep going, you're doing something amazing.

WORD SEARCH

Find the words listed below and circle them.

R	G	B	E	S	S	E	N	T	I	A	L
S	D	V	A	M	H	N	T	S	C	E	S
H	B	R	W	J	E	W	B	G	T	S	K
Y	A	E	S	K	A	R	A	H	Y	F	J
P	C	N	D	I	T	R	G	J	U	A	Q
T	K	C	G	S	P	A	R	E	P	T	F
E	U	R	S	N	A	C	K	S	N	R	W
R	P	D	H	T	D	D	P	O	U	C	H
M	I	R	R	O	R	S	D	H	R	T	Y

- ESSENTIAL
- BAG
- SPARE
- BACKUP
- HEATPAD
- POUCH
- SNACK
- MIRROR
- EMERGENCY

GLOSSARY

Menstruation	The medical word for your period—the time when blood leaves your body from the uterus.
Uterus	A muscle in your lower belly where your period starts—it builds and sheds lining each month.
Ovary	You've got two! They release eggs each month and make important hormones like estrogen.
Ovulation	The moment each month when an ovary releases an egg.
Cramps	Those achy feelings in your lower belly when your uterus contracts during your period.
Prostaglandins	The body chemicals that cause cramps by making the uterus tighten and squeeze.
Discharge	A white or clear fluid that comes from your vagina—totally normal and keeps things clean.

Estrogen	A hormone that helps your body go through puberty and keeps your cycle going.
Progesterone	Another hormone that works with estrogen to control your period and mood.
Vagina	The inside part of your body where period blood comes out (and where tampons go in).
Vulva	The outside part—includes your labia, clitoris, and vaginal opening.
PMS	Stands for Premenstrual Syndrome—a mix of mood swings and body changes before your period.
Cycle	The full length of time from the start of one period to the next—usually about 28 days.
Flow	How much blood comes out during your period—can be light, medium, or heavy.
Period Kit	A little bag with supplies like pads, wipes, and spare underwear—your secret period weapon!

Bloating	A feeling of fullness or swelling in the stomach area that can happen before or during a period.
Discharge	Normal fluid from the vagina that helps keep it clean and healthy.
Endometrium	The lining inside the uterus that thickens and sheds during a menstrual cycle.
Fatigue	Feeling very tired or low on energy.
Follicle	A tiny sac in the ovary that holds and releases an egg.
Growth Spurt	A time when the body grows taller or changes quickly during puberty.
Inflammation	When part of the body becomes swollen or sensitive, sometimes causing pain.
Spotting	Light bleeding that can happen before or after a period.

PERIOD
Tracker

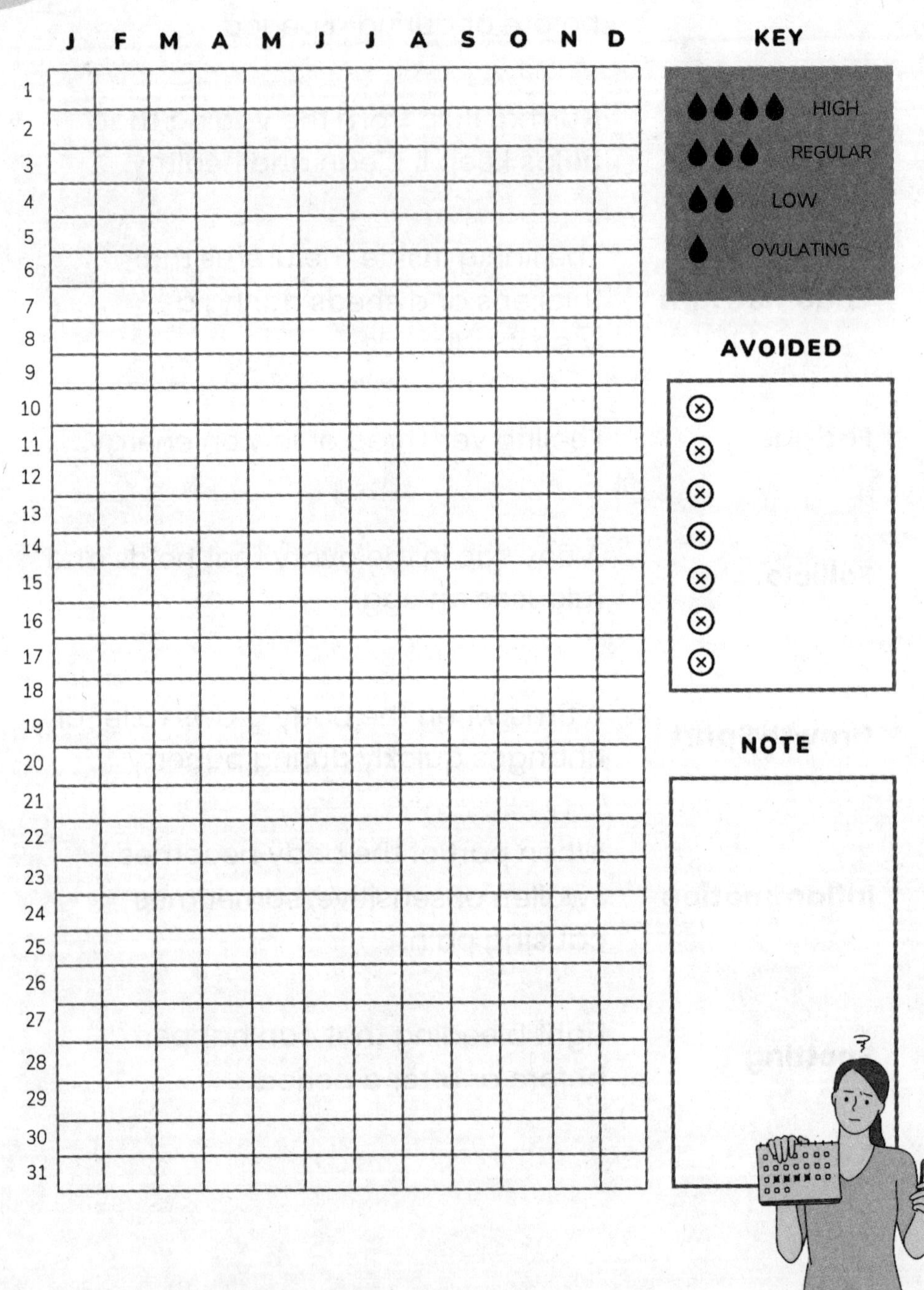

MONTH: ____________ YEAR: __________

30 DAY MOOD TRACKER

DAY 1

DAY 2

DAY 3

DAY 4

DAY 5

DAY 6

DAY 7

DAY 8

DAY 9

DAY 10

DAY 11

DAY 12

DAY 13

DAY 14

DAY 15

DAY 16

DAY 17

DAY 18

DAY 19

DAY 20

DAY 21

DAY 22

DAY 23

DAY 24

DAY 25

DAY 26

DAY 27

DAY 28

DAY 29

DAY 30

NOTES

MONTH: ____________ YEAR: ____________

30 DAY MOOD TRACKER

DAY 1
DAY 2
DAY 3
DAY 4
DAY 5
DAY 6
DAY 7
DAY 8
DAY 9
DAY 10
DAY 11
DAY 12
DAY 13
DAY 14
DAY 15

DAY 16
DAY 17
DAY 18
DAY 19
DAY 20
DAY 21
DAY 22
DAY 23
DAY 24
DAY 25
DAY 26
DAY 27
DAY 28
DAY 29
DAY 30

NOTES

MONTH: ____________ YEAR: __________

30 DAY MOOD TRACKER

DAY 1

DAY 2

DAY 3

DAY 4

DAY 5

DAY 6

DAY 7

DAY 8

DAY 9

DAY 10

DAY 11

DAY 12

DAY 13

DAY 14

DAY 15

DAY 16

DAY 17

DAY 18

DAY 19

DAY 20

DAY 21

DAY 22

DAY 23

DAY 24

DAY 25

DAY 26

DAY 27

DAY 28

DAY 29

DAY 30

NOTES

MONTH: ____________ YEAR: ________

30 DAY MOOD TRACKER

DAY 1

DAY 2

DAY 3

DAY 4

DAY 5

DAY 6

DAY 7

DAY 8

DAY 9

DAY 10

DAY 11

DAY 12

DAY 13

DAY 14

DAY 15

DAY 16

DAY 17

DAY 18

DAY 19

DAY 20

DAY 21

DAY 22

DAY 23

DAY 24

DAY 25

DAY 26

DAY 27

DAY 28

DAY 29

DAY 30

NOTES

MONTH: ____________ YEAR: ________

30 DAY MOOD TRACKER

DAY 1

DAY 2

DAY 3

DAY 4

DAY 5

DAY 6

DAY 7

DAY 8

DAY 9

DAY 10

DAY 11

DAY 12

DAY 13

DAY 14

DAY 15

DAY 16

DAY 17

DAY 18

DAY 19

DAY 20

DAY 21

DAY 22

DAY 23

DAY 24

DAY 25

DAY 26

DAY 27

DAY 28

DAY 29

DAY 30

NOTES

MONTH: ____________ YEAR: ____________

30 DAY MOOD TRACKER

DAY 1

DAY 2

DAY 3

DAY 4

DAY 5

DAY 6

DAY 7

DAY 8

DAY 9

DAY 10

DAY 11

DAY 12

DAY 13

DAY 14

DAY 15

DAY 16

DAY 17

DAY 18

DAY 19

DAY 20

DAY 21

DAY 22

DAY 23

DAY 24

DAY 25

DAY 26

DAY 27

DAY 28

DAY 29

DAY 30

NOTES

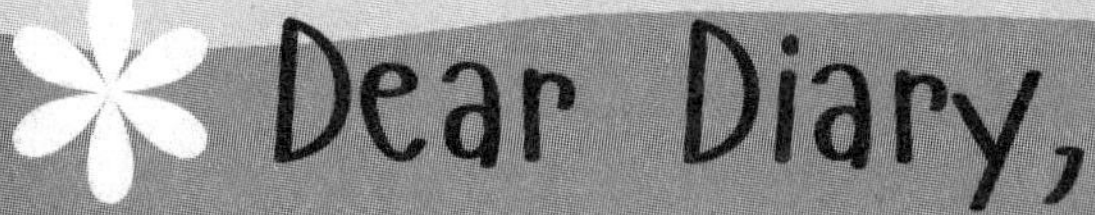

What superhero power would you give yourself during your period?

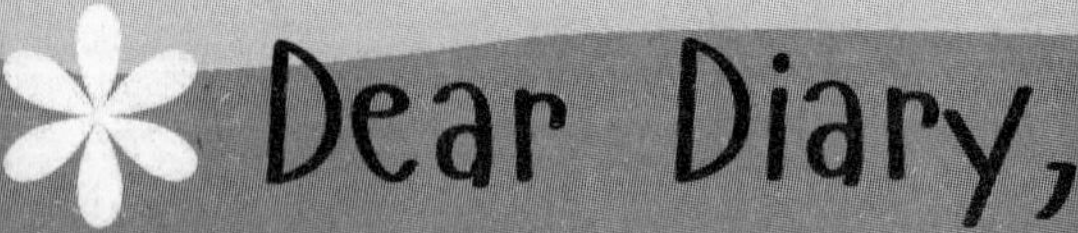

Dear Diary,

What's your favorite thing to do when you're on your period to make yourself feel better?

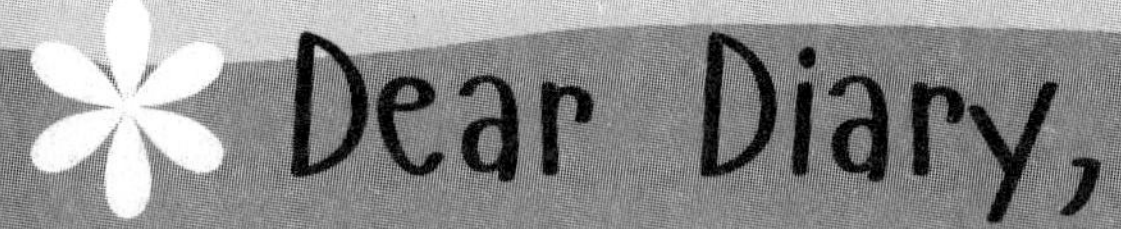

How would you explain your period to a friend who's never had one before?

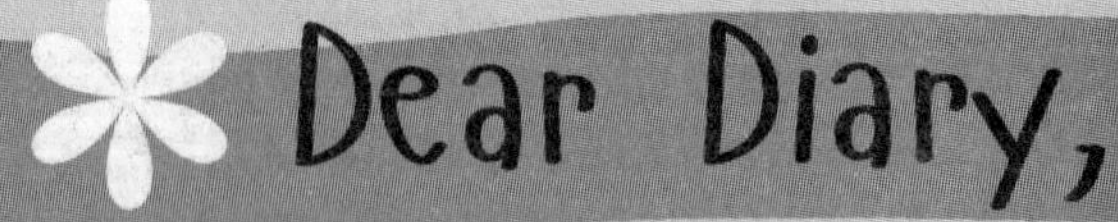

Make a list of the fun items you would put in your "Period Survival Kit."

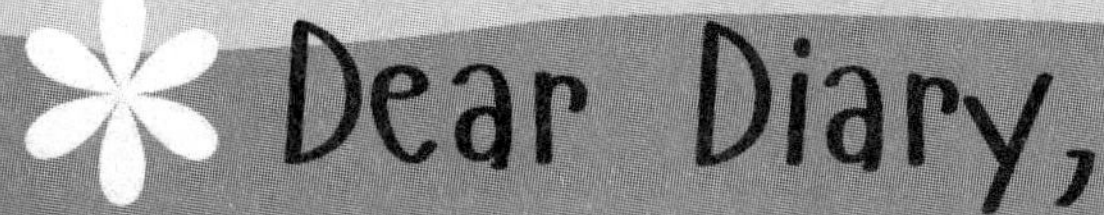

Imagine your period is a movie. What would the title be? Write the opening scene!

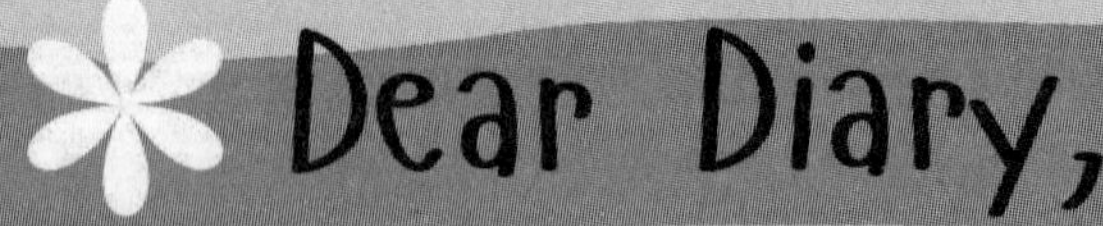

Dear Diary,

How do you feel about growing up? What's exciting about it, and what makes you laugh?

Dear Diary,

Describe your favorite "period outfit." What makes it comfy?

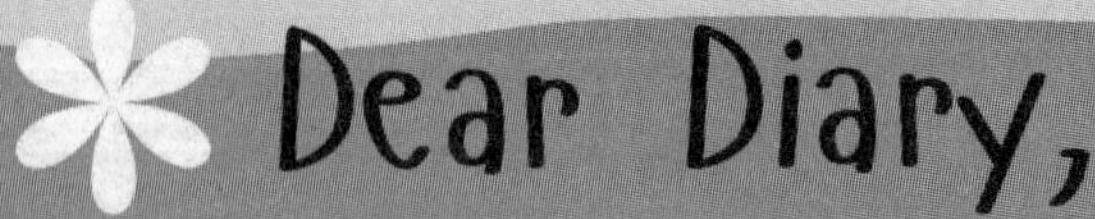

If your cramps could talk, what would they say? Write their funny dialogue.

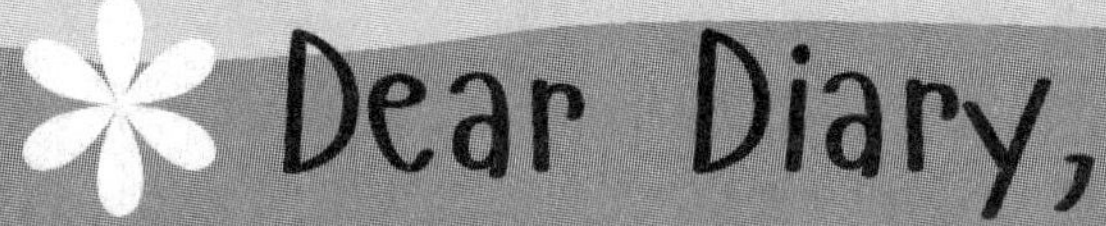

Create your own "period playlist" of things that cheer you up!

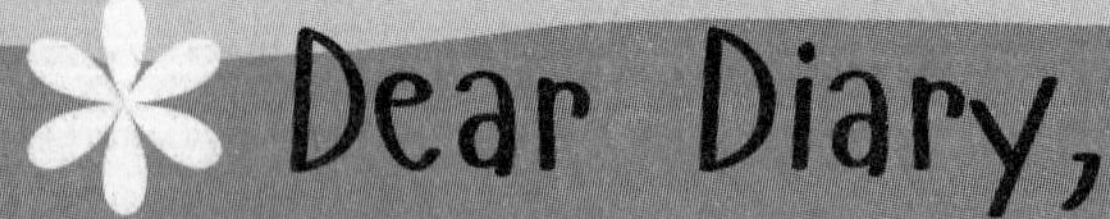

If your period could take you on a vacation, where would you go? Describe the trip!

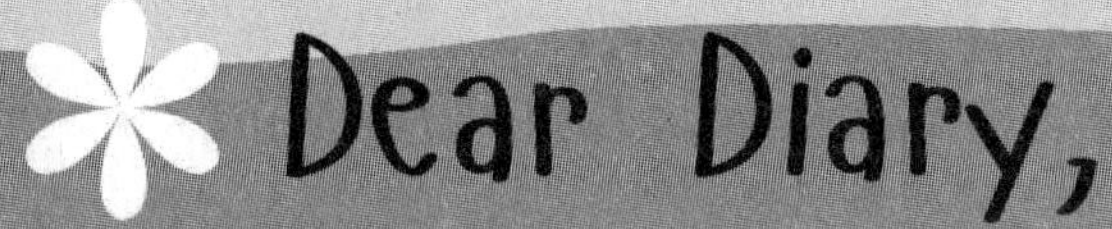

What's something you've learned that made you feel more confident about your body?

Write a letter to your future self about how you handle your period.

Dear Diary,

What's the funniest thing someone has said to you about periods? How did you respond?

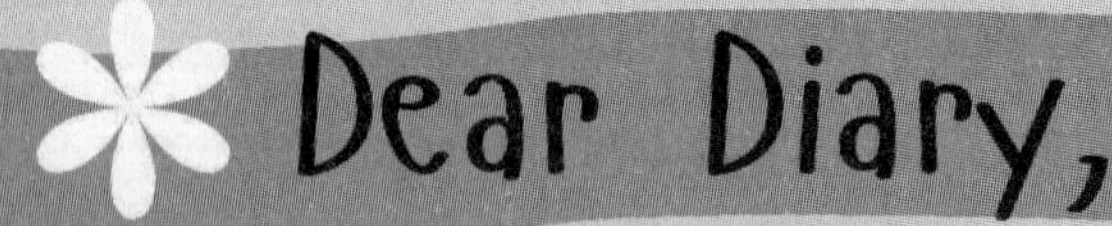

Write a fun poem about your period. It could be silly, empowering, or even a little dramatic!

Dear Diary,

What's a fun period fact you've learned that made you say, "Wow, I didn't know that!"?

What's your go-to snack or drink when you're on your period and why?

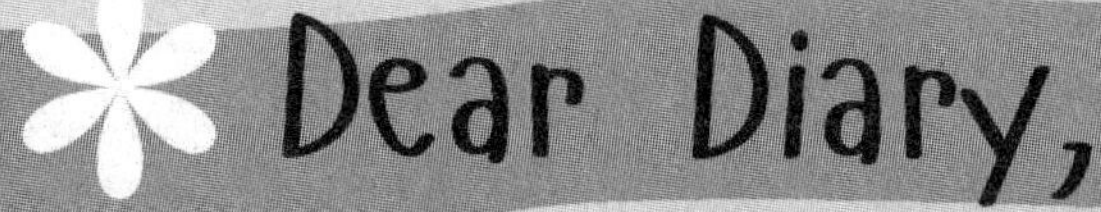

Write about a time when you asked for help during your period. How did it make you feel?

Dear Diary,

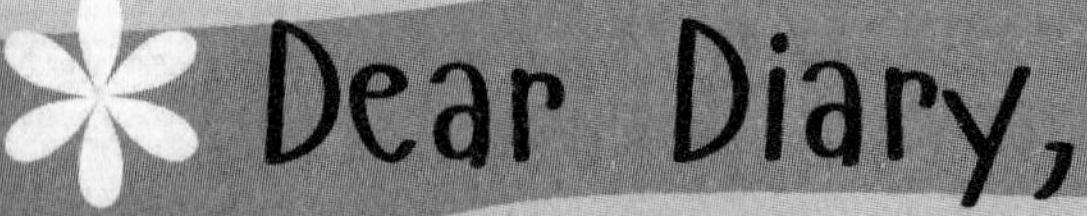

How do you feel about mood swings during your period? What helps you stay balanced?

Dear Diary,

If you could pick a theme song for your period, what would it be? Write the lyrics!

Dear Diary,

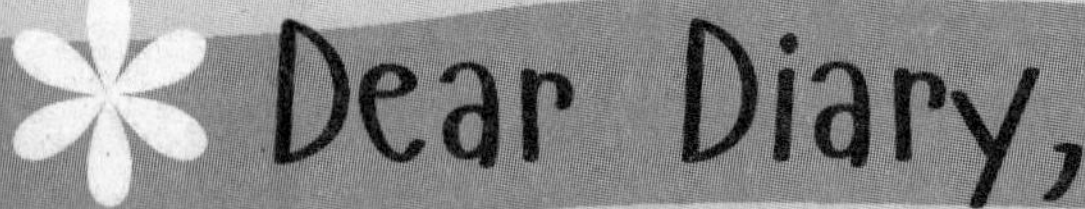

Imagine you could talk to your uterus.
Write a conversation between you and your body.

Get Your Free E-book

Get Your Free E-book
Scan the QR code below to instantly access the e-book
'My Growing-Up Journal', absolutely free

https://bonus.grapevinebooks.com/growingupjournal